I0191983

BORN TO WIN

Apostle Steve Lyston

Born To Win

Library of Congress Control Number: 2018906609
ISBN: 978-1-7320-7620-4

Edited by: Marsha A. McCormack and Michelle R. Lyston
Cover Design by: Johann D. A. Williams

This book was printed in the United States of America

Born To Win

DEDICATION

This book is dedicated to all those who are going through problems and extreme situations and to those who feel like giving up. There is always hope. Never give up. It is not about how you see yourself; it is about how God sees you! Never use your present circumstances to decide your future. You are one connection away from victory. Because you were *Born To Win* you cannot lose!

THANK YOUs

All thanks and honor to the Holy Spirit of God Who continues to strengthen, guide and teach us Wisdom.

Thank you to my wife Michelle, my children – Shevado, Hannah and Joshua for their continued support and love.

Thank you to Bishop Dr. Doris Hutchinson, for her unceasing prayer and support.

Thank you to the RWOMI Family for your genuine support and prayers.

CONTENTS

FOREWORD

Life comes with innumerable challenges and it is sometimes very hard to see beyond the problems we face. Oftentimes it is difficult for some of us to rise after a fall, or to pick up the proverbial pieces and move on after a loss of any kind; and the challenge intensifies when we are discouraged in the face of the challenges and can't understand why we must face these issues of life.

Further to all this, *change* is a word that many don't like to hear. In fact, they fight against this word in their lives on a daily basis, yet change has the potential to bring their greatest victory, especially if they embrace the Word and will of God in their lives.

Born To Win allows each reader to recognize that obstacles can become stepping stones and problems can actually be opportunities in disguise.

Born To Win allows the reader the opportunity to renew his/her mind and encourages him/her to look beyond the circumstances they physically see, remain focused and continue to move forward.

Read, and embrace the fact that you were *Born To Win*!

Pastor Dr. Michelle Lyston
Restoration World Outreach Ministries Inc.

PREFACE

This book was written to help the reader recognize that each life – their life - has purpose whether they realize it or not and that the challenges that come on a daily basis is not there to destroy a person, but to help to build them up and direct them to realizing and fulfilling their purpose. It can be used as a daily devotional and can be a source of encouragement in difficult times.

As you read this book, it will help to bring you to the next level, and cause you to realize and embrace the fact that you were *Born To Win*.

INTRODUCTION

Born To Win is inspired by the Holy Spirit to help us in our daily struggles. Sometimes we fall, but God wants us to rise up. We should never give up, regardless of the struggles we face. God has given a vision. There is purpose in each of us, but there will be obstacles and hindrances we must overcome when we are running the race.

Many things will come against us, illness, financial lack, betrayal and they all come to set us back. But God uses it to propel and promote us. You can overcome, because you were **Born To Win**! Never, never give up. It is not about how you see yourself. It is about how God sees you.

There are different strategies in this book, and it starts with the daily renewing of your mind. It will also require you having a clean heart, and your recognizing that there are miracles and power in your mouth. God also gives us the power to get wealth and we must embrace that as well. He gives us power to be rich, not only on a financial level, but also rich in His Spirit.

Understand that when you are rejected by men and seen as a societal outcast because of your difference, it means that there is greatness within you and that God is about to bring it to the fore to use you.

Chapter 1

EMBRACE CHANGE

Many locally and globally, and in particular the poor, are crying out for change. They want changes economically, governmentally and in all sectors. You too desire change. But are we really ready for change?

Change can come in different ways. Each season brings different opportunities and different kinds and levels of access. But in order for change to come, we must first be willing to change. Are we ready to change our mindset and our way of thinking in order to allow change to come?

Romans 12 tells us to renew our minds and begin to review our attitudes, motives and identify the basis of our foundation; to see on what is our foundation built?

Many say they want to see things change, but they are unwilling to change because they don't believe they need to change. Some are looking to their inner circle; some are looking at/to the strength of their empire and others to the military or their economy. However, we must all recognize that anything that is *not* built on the foundation of God, and if our trust is not in God, then we will crumble in a season of paradigm shifts. Are we willing to look at our stewardship and our communication skills?

Many leaders will not experience positive change unless they are willing to do something different. We all have to put our faith in action, particularly regarding Crime Reduction, Law and Order and the Economy. We all need to learn from King Ahasuerus who sought wise counsel in order to understand Times, Seasons, Laws and Justice in order to maintain integrity within his Administration. He started the change within His household first. (Esther 1)

The wise counselors knew that Leadership involves serious responsibilities, and that when one ignores his responsibilities then it is time for a change. If the king did not make the change necessary, then it would have cost him his kingship.

Communication

In our daily communication as leaders we must be willing first to listen to persons at all levels; especially to those below us. Every leader should learn and employ the communication skills used by Jesus! Jesus listened even to the prostitute who was a significant influence in His ministry. Not only did Jesus communicate with the then elite in the mountains, but He also communicated with the common man in the plains! He communicated clearly so that they could understand without being or sounding condescending to the people. Most leaders today do not communicate for the normal man to understand; they simply use jargon and terminologies that only those within their circles understand – and barely so. Unless leaders begin improving their communication skills (Mark 12: 37; Luke 6: 17; Matthew 5: 1) then they are going to be swept away in the change.

The Church and the Secular Industries

In order to have and maintain positive changes, the Church and the Secular Industries need to unite to deal with the problems ahead. A prime example of this occurred with Joseph and Pharaoh. They both had to unite so that Egypt could remain strong during the famine, so much so that other nations would come to them for help during the economic hardship. Likewise, Joseph had to adapt to the Egyptian culture while staying true to God.

Planning and Discipline are key elements when it comes to change! We have to plan ahead for good times and bad. We must have empty rooms for expansion and filled rooms in the event of bad times. We must also have the discipline to maintain it all, and to be effective in this year of change.

We must learn from the ants who can teach us to be industrious; from the rock badger who will teach us how to survive; the locust, who teaches us how to cooperate even if there is no leader; and the spider, who will teach us how to accomplish through consistency! We need to begin recording our goals and objectives for the positive change that we require. But God must be the center of our plans. Never resist positive change.

Changes will bring us out of our comfort zones, but it will also bring out of us the hidden gifts and potentials that are within us.

Born To Win

If negative change happens, then know that it may very well be an opportunity that is opening up for positive changes to take place for you.

Prepare for Change

Nothing remains the same. Everything is changing including the earth. Times change. Seasons change. Mankind is the only being that resists change.

Change is inevitable, but there are many who say that everything must be proven and that beyond that it is either not real or not worth knowing. However, if that is the belief in the season of change, then many will be humbled, and they will no longer experience favor! If what they believe is true, then how do we prove that there is a tomorrow?

Those who plan without God are in fact proclaiming that they are their own masters. Every sector has to prepare for change – politicians, media, church, business investors and every other sector. If persons within these sectors don't plan, then there are going to be great losses and numerous missed opportunities.

Some are praying for God to move, but when God moves, if we are not willing to change our mindsets and follow His leading then we will miss the mark.

Many nations are suffering because every time we are given the opportunity for change they make the wrong choices. Choices always bring us either forward or backward. What are you willing to do differently? Are you willing to change your way of thinking? Are you willing to be criticized and to stand alone in order to get the right results?

In order to understand change, we must be sensitive to His word. It is critical for us to recognize the season we are in and what that season requires. We must ask the question, 'How do I deal with those who resist change?'

Every leader must be sensitive to Times and Seasons. If they are not, then the wise thing to do is to surround themselves with those who do.

Many leaders still think that the old tricks of the trade will always work but they don't. Are we willing to embrace God's principles to help humanity and to bring change? Are they willing to implement new strategies and plans, restructure and reform?

Market Conditions

Failure to understand the changes in Market Conditions and even the general marketplace itself is the driving force behind our global problems. Most financial institutions do not understand Times and Seasons and so many of them are caught off-guard, which causes great suffering to humanity.

It is time for the Government and the financial institutions to deal with this issue and change their leadership styles and approach.

Many people and nations often respond to situations after the fact rather than putting plans in place in the event of a situation? This can bring failure, loss and waste. When one does not plan for change, then they get changed!

For countries that do not have an economic blueprint or practical strategies in place, but instead depend on other countries' or organization's policies to drive their nation's economy, they need to ask and answer very serious questions. 'How will my country (and countrymen) respond to changes that occur within that other nation (or organization); how will those changes negatively affect my country?' 'What contingency plans have been put in place to deal with major changes and/or fallouts within the other nation?'

It is better to build a foundation ahead of time that can deal with the potential changes ahead and expand where necessary; than to attempt a clean up after things have gone awry.

Many things take place in a season of change – a changing of the guard, market change, variety, systems, legislation, monetary policies, prices, climate change, security, shift and people.

Changes can come about through uncommon people and in uncommon places, through uncommon situations.

Sometimes, the greatest access we receive comes when we are willing to change according to His Times and Seasons. It is important for us to recognize that the most problematic areas or situations within a nation are where the greatest wealth exists.

We must be willing to embrace and be a part of the change necessary for individual and national development and success; and to do this requires us to prepare ourselves for inevitable change.

We Need To Change Our Speech

A great deal of negativity exists in the world today, so that when someone says something kind or positive, we find it difficult to simply receive it.

So, for example, if someone says: 'Have a beautiful day' or 'It's going to be a beautiful day', the response to that will include – 'What's so beautiful about it?'.

Is Negativity Around You?

Negativity has been dominating the world and many, especially the social media, have become driven by negativity.

2 Corinthians 4:13 says: "And since we have the same spirit of faith, according to what is written, 'I believed and therefore I spoke', we also believe and therefore speak."

Words form, shape, create; and what we believe is what we speak. So, if you believe you were born for greatness, never stop believing and always keep speaking it.

Positive confessions release God's will and purpose in the earth and if you don't confess what you are hoping for, you might not possess it.

Negative confessions agree with the enemy concerning the bad things that are being spoken about you. (Matthew 12: 33-37)

Oftentimes, the bad things that happen are a result of the negative things spoken about oneself. So, if, for example, you believe and speak – "things will never change" or "things will never get better", or when we say, "man, business is just bad," – then that is exactly what will happen.

Words Can Heal or Hurt

If we are going to change our environment and change our circumstances, we will need to change our speech. The words you speak determine your future. Words bring edification or defilement. Positive words bring health and life. Oral confessions declare, confirm and seal the belief of the heart.

Negative and bad words affect the environment negatively. If they truly want to see change, then the media and social networks have to change their speech and focus.

Negative words send poison into the atmosphere which brings uncleanness. When God is going to bring change to a city or a nation, the first thing he does is change the speech of the people.

Negative words open the door for other things happening. In Numbers 13, the negative focus and complaints of the 10 of 12 spies sent to investigate the potential for forward movement and upward mobility, opened the door for fear, unbelief, doubt, murder, division and hopelessness of a people.

Negative words are contagious and bring extreme discouragement. There are times when people may be going through hard times, but they need encouragement more than money sometimes.

So if the news is continually negative, the media focus solely on the negative and the people constantly hear and express negativity, then what do we think will result?

Negative words bring serious wounds. People recover more quickly from physical abuse than from verbal abuse.

Focus on the Positive

We must endeavor to speak and focus on the positive.

Has anyone ever told you: "It just can't happen" or "It will never work."? Have you heard, "You will never have a child", "You will never make it to the top", "You will never amount to anything good"?

All these are curses, and when people speak these things about you, don't embrace them, reject those words immediately.

Declare these words daily and watch your mountains crumble.

I decree good news today. Favor and grace shall be my portion. I decree change in my community. I declare increase in sales and profit margins. I decree promotion for me today. I declare that I am righteous and holy.

I decree that righteous leaders will begin to come forth. I decree crime reduction, divine tactics and strategy for crime reduction. I decree and declare debt write-offs and debt cancellations daily.

I decree comprehensive and divine direction.

Wealth and riches shall be in my house. Purity and tranquility shall be in my borders. Order and stability shall take place. I decree restoration of my family and other families, and covering for the children playing in the streets and those going to school. I decree that the airwaves and the print media will bring positive influence and change within every community.

I decree waivers from Government and that money will come into my account from unusual sources. I decree that the natural and human resources will begin to come forth and remain within this nation. I declare that I will create witty inventions. I declare healing for me, my family and my nation, in Jesus' name. Amen.

Philosophic Views Don't Bring Change

There is a great fight globally for political power. Even those who have failed badly are fighting for dear life to stay in power! Over the years successive leaders have made promises and many of them were simply not kept. A total generation of youth have been robbed of their inheritance! Hopelessness has crept in, while many are fighting to leave a political legacy. While many want to bring change, real change can only come when the strongholds over the minds of the people are pulled down or broken!

We cannot bring change by using physical methods or strategies. Neither can winning an election – by fair means or foul – bring true change! Carnal weapons consist of those which are man-made devices which are philosophic strongholds! Fear, deception, lies, reverse psychology, intimidation and manipulation (especially of the language) are some of these devices. Every effort man makes external to the Cross will bring failure!

When we utilize the principle of Christ to bring down strongholds, the Holy Spirit will bring victory! Carnal and worldly weapons will not do it. Weapons empowered by God are what bring changes.

Strongholds are first established in the mind and behind every stronghold there is a lie and behind every lie there is fear; behind every fear there is an idol! Idols are established whenever there exists a failure to trust in the provision of God which are ours through Jesus Christ.

Some of the weapons that bring down strongholds are:

- ✓ God's Word – Hebrews 4: 12 – 13

- ✓ The Blood of Jesus – Revelation 12: 11

- ✓ The Name of Jesus – Mark 16: 17

- ✓ Praise and Worship\t- II Chronicles 20: 20 – 30

- ✓ Fasting – Ezra 8: 21 / Ezra 9: 5

- ✓ Repentance – Joel 1 & 2

- ✓ Weeping and Wailing\t – II Chronicles 7: 14

- ✓ Strongholds must be confronted and pulled down. (Ephesians 6: 13 – 18 & Jeremiah 1: 5)

After the Children of Israel were delivered by God through Moses from oppression and bondage, it was strongholds that caused them to once again desire Egypt and the things of Egypt. Strongholds of their minds caused them to use the very thing that was to keep them out of debt in the Land of Promise, to create the idol they chose to worship.

When people sell their votes or vote based on mere benefits and food, it is the result of strongholds! Esau sold and thus lost his birthright because he gave in to his temporary situation for a plate of food!
Leaders Must Inquire

Hopelessness, Crime, Fear, Failure, Violence, Unemployment, Immorality, the killing of our children, the famine cannot be dealt with by simply using man's intellect!

If any leader wants to deal with the above issues, as David did in 2 Samuel 21: 1 – 14, then they must be bold enough, as David was, to inquire of the Lord. They must be willing to face the truth and call a time of repentance.

Which leader is bold enough to call a time of repentance and actually repent not just for the nation but also for the mistakes of past Administrations on all sides? When we find that leader, then we will see change!

If any leader or nation wants to experience peace, or they desire to see change within, or get political victory, then it means that things must be done God's way! One can also victory by using the wrong methods; but what are the consequences? Wrong methods always brings severe consequences!

Any leader who is willing to genuinely call upon God will be assured of victory! They don't even have to fight in the battle, God will raise up someone around them who will take the giants down!
There is no such thing as a one man army!

Diverting from God's Word Brings Problems

God is the Master of Tactics and Strategies! He is the Ultimate Strategist and One of Immense Wisdom and Knowledge! As such, simply relying on human brain power to resolve matters and bring change is simply unwise!

We must remember that excluding God keeps the solutions we need at bay! We must be willing to consult the ultimate strategist! God.

Change Your Focus for What Lies Ahead

Many have gone through pain, delay, disappointment and even loss of loved ones, but we must remain grateful to the One Who created us all. Many from the start of the year made resolutions; some we gained, some we lost. Each of us has our season that we go through and sometimes these seasons come to strengthen our faith and to change our focus and priority. The time has come for us to evaluate our list – check off what was accomplished, what was not and formulate a new list of goals for the year ahead.

Believe by faith that there is an opportunity for the things that did not happen for you in the past will happen for you right now. God *is* faithful and He always keeps His promises. It is us as human beings who tend not to keep our promises. When we are reviewing our past, let us do an honest evaluation and identification of our shortfalls. We need to ask ourselves, 'What were my shortfalls and what can I do differently to bring change?'

But don't dwell on the shortfalls and past mistakes and challenges. Just simply recognize that they are only your platforms to greater things.

In order to bring change, *we* first must change. Many times, people make resolutions but are unwilling to change although they need a change! So we need to ask ourselves some questions:

- ✓ Was I a good steward of the little with which God entrusted me?
- ✓ Did I manage my money and time properly?
- ✓ Did I use the gifts and talents God has given me to bring positive change to someone else's life?
- ✓ Did I volunteer to help my community?
- ✓ Did I go to the House of the Lord faithfully this year?

✓ Was God first in my life; did I spend enough time with Him this year?

✓ After I got that new job/promotion, did I give God thanks?

✓ What were the things that 'stressed me out' in the past?

✓ What areas were/Who was my greatest focus?

We must answer honestly if we are to get our desired change.

Moving Forward

Going forward we need to change our focus:

✓ We must manage our time even better
✓ We need to invest in those people who make us happy
✓ We need to cut off those that suck your energy without valuing our time
✓ We need to place a value on ourselves and set the value standard for those around us
✓ We need to build ourselves an inner circle of good strong supporters

Then pray and ask the Lord to reveal to you the Times and Seasons and what needs to be done going forward. Ask Him what your focus for the year(s) ahead must be and we have to change our focus toward that. Oftentimes we believe that the year we enter will be like the year we are leaving behind and it is not so. For some things to change there must be the internal change to receive the external changes. For example, you may need your finance to increase, your healing and your relationship within your family to change, but your answer may lie in your committing yourself to Jesus Christ as your Lord and Savior. Maybe we also have to change the way we eat and maintain it so that we can have a better quality of life. Some will need to stop 'shacking up', because our bodies are the temple of the Lord.

There needs to be greater focus on the children and their welfare and education; who influences them, who is their focus, what are their values, what are they watching. As parents, we *must* manage. It is not the responsibility of the Government to manage our children it is ours.

Stop unnecessary spending, God wants each person to own a debt-free house.

Seek God first going forward, not the Social Media and the opinions shared there. It is not FOX News, CNN or Market Conditions that should be the determining factors for our decision-making. Judge all things to see whether or not it lines up with what God is saying to you.

Never try to change or appease anyone, only God can do that. Please God and God will please the people.

The voices with which you surround yourself will determine your success in 2017. There are many voices out there and many 'truths' out there, but only one real Truth. Many ways, but only one is the right way.

Chapter 2

MENTORSHIP: AN IMPORTANT KEY TO SUCCESS

Mentorship vs. Manipulation

There is a fine line between Mentorship and Manipulation and sadly many have been burnt by the latter on their road to success. The failure/lack of success that we are seeing globally, is the result of the lack of proper mentorship and the abundance of manipulation. It is therefore necessary for us to recognize that Mentorship guides and matures a person into greatness and fulfillment of their purpose for the benefit of all; while Manipulation directs a person to a path through exploitation, deception and control in order to maintain or access power – thus the only beneficiary is the person directing. Sadly, manipulation does not only occur in politics, media, and business, but also within churches across the globe.

Mentorship

A mentor is a trustworthy counselor of guide who would teach or advise a less experienced or less knowledgeable person. Your mentor can be older or younger than you are, because mentorship is dependent on the level of expertise, experience and/knowledge in a particular area.

The focus of mentorship is to develop the *whole* person so that one can mature to be used in a greater capacity.

We need mentorship in politics, religion, business, media, Security Forces, and the Church. The transmission of knowledge can be formal or informal.

In carrying out mentorship, one can use experience with insight from the Holy Spirit. One can also use their experience from pain and passion. It is a process that means you will need to walk side by side with the learner to bring fruit. There are things that will develop that you can only learn along the way with your protégé/mentee. A mentor should never be afraid to pass on knowledge to develop an individual; there are always benefits for both parties.

We have seen the withholding of knowledge from one generation to the next which is a failure on the part of those who should be mentors. Many organizations are now dying because there is a lack of mentorship and an abundance of manipulation. Your mentor will give you insight, tactics and strategies and wisdom to launch and be successful globally. In the Bible we see great mentors and great protégés/mentees. For example:

Mentors	Protégés/Mentees
Naomi	Ruth
Elijah	Elisha
Mordecai	Esther

Every protégé/mentee must follow those who have proven themselves and have overcome life's struggles. Do not follow someone only because/if they are financially successful. Follow one who has a wealth of knowledge, the fear of God, strong, positive moral values.

Your mentor will teach you the Law of Access, Protocol for the environment in which you are preparing to go, and even how to dress for where you are headed. Recognize that your mentor also has the authority to speak you into your success and onto your path of prosperity!

There cannot be any economic development or global change until strong mentors rise up and begin to challenge the people toward development. When we see the young and the old competing with each other in politics and in the churches, then it is clear that there is a failure in the area of mentorship.

Remember that the key to mentorship is **the right motive**! Your mentors are there to prevent you from any unnecessary pain, mistakes or failures. They are also there to bring out your true potential; and to address your pitfalls which hinder you, such as pride, arrogance and zeal without knowledge. The mentor is preparing you for both the blessing and the enemy ahead.

The success of a leader must be measured by the number of lives they have impacted and have empowered and raised up to be leaders as well, so that there is continuation. This principle is in line with the Biblical instruction from God to '… be fruitful and multiply…' (Genesis 1: 28)

I truly believe that nations need to start setting up Schools of Mentorship, where they pull people from every sector who would empower and pass on the wisdom and knowledge they have gained in their areas of expertise. These schools must be open to all! No qualification limits must be put on who will attend these schools. You may find that those who attend may choose a different and more positive career path; which could ultimately reduce crime.

Manipulation

Manipulation is about wielding power and control. Manipulation directs a person to a path through exploitation, deception and control in order to maintain or access power. It comes in many ways and in different arenas.

Manipulation exists in politics, religion, media, business, education, our social lives and even in marriage! It is the greatest hindrance right now regarding good governance and advancing a nation's growth. If, for example, an individual believes that they are academically superior to you, then they will make efforts to manipulate you in order to maintain or wield power over you. That is why there is no great effort to reduce effort properly.

Manipulation in the Church

Within the Church, the level of manipulation is so high that the 'regular' Christian does not truly know what it is to be a real Christian. There are 2 basic types of manipulation happening in the Church:

1. The Charismatic/Pentecostal Manipulation
2. The Traditional Church Manipulation

The Charismatic/Pentecostal Manipulation occurs where people utilize their gifts to manipulate people and ultimately shift them out of their purpose, because they want to maintain control and dominion over them. They pull the believer from Christ and pull them to themselves; teaching them about a Crown without the Cross! They utilize the Scriptures such as II Chronicles 20: 20 or Amos 3: 7, for example, and they manipulate the meaning of that Scripture to influence people to listen to them only and shift from the true meaning of that Word. However, if we examine those Scriptures, we will see the word 'His' before the words 'prophets' and 'servants'. What if the prophet is not of God?

The Traditional Church Manipulation employs the use of Theology and Philosophy to keep the people in a state of spiritual blindness and ignorance, as well as spiritual passivity! They often engage in heresy, promising progressive Christianity where Christ is demoted and the basic tenets of Christianity are negated or ignored. They choose to ignore the Holy Spirit and His work especially in present time, and confine His existence only to the time of Scriptures. They focus on the Law/Legalism instead of Grace as principles for daily living (Colossians 2: 8); they promise enlightenment and liberation when in fact, by virtue of ignoring and belittling the work of the Holy Spirit in present time, they bring people deeper in bondage spiritually and mentally and keep the people dependent on them, much like the Pharisees of Biblical times. Instead they invite magicians and New Age principles and activities (such as Yoga) into the House of the Lord.

Manipulation in Business and Politicians

In business, especially in Sales and Market Research, they will withhold information from you, ask you what you are looking for and try to find out how knowledgeable you are of their inner workings. Then they steer you in a particular direction and lock you into a deal. By the time the true picture is revealed, you have already signed.

Many lawyers use our ignorance/lack of knowledge of the law, and manipulate the meanings or words and terminologies to manipulate and rob us with our eyes wide open! Many of those in that profession who are called brilliant and genius, are in fact some of the greatest manipulators.

The politicians use eloquence in oration (pretty speeches) to manipulate, and many listening use it as an indication of the speaker's intelligence, knowledge and academic achievement; they also assume that it means they are good and care deeply about their listeners, and those politicians know that! A person's eloquence does not indicate whether they will be good leaders or not.

Individual Manipulation

At the individual level, manipulators cause you to feel guilty should you disagree with or try to pull away from them. They always remind you of what they did for you in the past. They will invite you to lunch, for example, and ask you probing questions. They want to carry out a SWOT Analysis of sorts on you before they make their move on you. In other words, they want to know your strengths and weaknesses to determine if you are a threat to them and see what opportunities exist with you. They want to know where you stand, so they will ask you: 'What do you think about X leader/person?'

For change to come, we need Mentorship, not Manipulation.

Mentors/Role Models – The Key To Your Success

As the nation experiences the continued disintegration of core values and principles that makes a nation strong, it is becoming clearer that what is needed is good mentors for those coming up to emulate and bring the nation back to where it was and make it what it ought to be. There is a serious lack of good mentors and we see it playing out in politics, business, the entertainment industry, sports and all other sectors within the nation.

There is a serious lack of respect all around coupled with the lack of proper mentors and it has created a vacuum which the dons and criminals are quickly filling up! That has led to an increase in the Crime situation and if good mentors/role models are missing, then our problems with crime and violence will continue to worsen!

One of the reasons the Church is not as effective and as influential as they ought to be is as a result of a lack of mentors/'fathers' in the Church. Paul in I Corinthians 4: 15 said "For though you might have ten thousand instructors in Christ, yet you do not have **many fathers**; for in Christ Jesus I have begotten you through the gospel." While an instructor will tell you what to do, a father teaches and guides you in the right way.

The Role of a Mentor

Now no earthly mentor is perfect, they all have weaknesses and strengths. The key thing, however, is too look for mentor who will tell you the truth – tell you like it is - whether it pleases you or not.

A mentor will:

- ✓ Bring out the dormant gift that is in you
- ✓ Cause influential people to listen to you
- ✓ Teach you protocol, including:
  - how to operate in a hostile environment and come out on top; and,
  - how to respect all those in authority

A mentor is honest with you about you and is interested in your prosperity, and can determine your wealth, success, promotion (Ruth 3: 1 – 5; Proverbs 4: 8 – 9).   They analyze and discern things in you that you cannot see.

They know your weaknesses and your limitations and are willing to push or pull you beyond that!   A mentor is *not* focused on being a friend, but rather on ensuring your success!

Many who have accomplished great things will tell you that they had good mentors. Today, we can still identify mentors that have and still can make a difference in young lives. In Business we can look at the impact that men such as Carlton Alexander, Maya Matalon and Aaron Matalon have made. Many shrewd business persons have come up through their hands including Dr. Douglas Orane, Former CEO of GraceKennedy Limited and former president of the Private Sector Organization of Jamaica (PSOJ).

In Sports, there are:

- ✓ Carl Brown – former Jamaican footballer, manager and coach
- ✓ Winston Chung-Fah – legendary football coach
- ✓ Ben Francis – Jamaican football legend
- ✓ Donald Quarrie – Jamaican top world sprinter 1970's
- ✓ Herb McKinley – Jamaican top world sprinter 1940's

and from them came persons such as

- ✓ Merlene Ottey,

- ✓ Grace Jackson-Small,
- ✓ Paul Young,
- ✓ Andrew Price and
- ✓ Lenword Hyde.

Some of these are now mentors.

In Politics it was the late Prime Minister, The Honorable Michael N. Manley, who mentored former Prime Ministers, the Honorable Percival J. Patterson and the Honorable Portia Simpson-Miller. Former Prime Minister of Jamaica, the Honorable Edward Seaga mentored the Minister of Finance Audley Shaw and Prime Minister of Jamaica, the Honorable Andrew Holness. Additionally, from the late Prime Minister, the Honorable Hugh Shearer came The Honorable Rudyard "Ruddy" Spencer – former Minister of Health.

Many successful persons will tell you that their greatest influencers were their teachers or principals. Our education system today seriously lacks teachers who are also positive role models who are not afraid to apply the whip! If we remove flogging from the school, the crime and security budgets and the health bill will increase!

Mentor to Manage

It would be remiss of me to speak about mentors without making mention of and giving proper due to persons who have positively influenced my life in various ways.

To the distinguished Jamaicans who mentored me - Joseph A. Matalon, Joseph M. Matalon, Colin Steele, Novar McDonald, Ryan White, Claudette Chin, Yvonne Johnson, Lloyd Tomlinson, Paul Marston, Bishop Doris Hutchinson, Herman Fennel Jr., Rev. Wayne Palmer, Lt. Col. Derrick Penso, Lt. Linton Gordon, Delroy Roach,

Beverley Chambers, Professor Neville Ying, F. C. Latty, Dennis O'Nash, Sgt. Maj. Leroy McKenzie, Sgt. Major Patrick Cabey, and Sgt. Maj. Byron Clarke, Sgt. Major George Flakes – Thank you!

For change to begin, we must each revisit those who have made a positive impact on our lives – thank them and then become positive roles model and a mentor for someone else.

Honor Determines Your Future

Many of the problems we are no facing in our society today is the result of a lack of honor and a great deal of dishonor to replace it. Honor begins within the home and regardless of the various systems different ones want to implement – whether the legal system, the New Age Movement or anyone else, the real change for better will not take place until honor and the value of honor is restored.

The Bible commands us to honor God, honor our parents, honor government, honor elders, honor leaders and honor widows. These are critical for blessings. The Bible reminds us that honor brings blessings and dishonor brings curses. If you want to see the levels of dishonor being shown on a daily basis, you can catch a quick glimpse of it on mainstream or social media. You will even see the level of dishonor being shown by columnists, lobbyists/social activists to honorable people. We need to recognize that even when people have fallen, you must honor them. Regardless of their political, social or

educational background, where honor is due it ought to be given. We have seen politicians being shown great dishonor publicly, for example, The Honorable Portia Simpson-Miller, The Honorable Bruce Golding and President Donald Trump. Even young politicians on the political platform showing dishonor with their disrespectful statements about their colleagues or opponents and the crowd would laugh or shout in support without realizing that the dishonor shown could cancel their very future.

When an activist even shows dishonor to a man of God and people laugh, even if the man of God is guilty, this can bring a curse and wipe out their future.

Growing up in the country, we dare not call an elder within the community a nickname. The entire community would discipline us. Today we see people dishonoring the police, teachers, each other and getting support from the society. Members of the police force also show levels of dishonor to the public and particularly to some elders in the public when they should stand up in reverence to them. One thing with the army, it is one of the few remaining institutions that teach people to honor. Every man has to pay compliment to each other. I pray they will never allow external factors and lobbyists to breakdown the system of honor that exists in the army.

Honor Church Leaders

Have you ever seen how people rhyme and mock church leaders, or even God's Word when it is pronounced? In the Bible, everyone that brings dishonor always

experiences retribution? David's wife Michal dishonored him by criticizing him – she became barren. Moses' sister dishonored him by criticizing him – she became plagued with leprosy. Elisha was dishonored by a group of youth who mocked him and called him names. They were killed – eaten by a bear.

The ineffectiveness of many intercessors within the Church is the result of dishonoring their leaders. Every good leader within the Church must receive double honor. (1 Timothy 5: 17) Praying for the church, the leaders and the nation while tearing them down, gossiping about and undermining them at the same time brings dishonor which brings hardship and suffering on many of them.

When leaders look down on or curse the poor, the weak and those with disabilities, then a curse is released on them (Leviticus 19: 14) "You shall not revile God, nor curse a ruler of your people." (Exodus 22: 28)

Blessings for Honor

Every successful person – whether in the Bible or in life today, has at some point in their life/walk/career has extended honor where it was due and has reaped the benefits of it.

- ✓ Honor promotes you and extends your life. It allows your borders to be extended and releases great blessings and deliverance. (1 Chronicles 4)

- ✓ Honor brings favor and direction, particularly to political leaders. If the leaders were honoring God by listening and obeying His Word we would not be on the path of decline we are con currently.

- ✓ Honor bring s great financial blessing. (Proverbs 3: 8 – 9) When we honor Him with the finance then great blessings will result.

- ✓ Honor brought a simple woman named Ruth, into becoming a billionaire by honoring her mentor Naomi. There are many men a women who are in great organizations – whether secular, church or political; but they are unable to receive from the leader they serve because they curse them on a daily basis. Some even expose their leaders in order to receive recognition.

✓ Never trust a person who doesn't honor their leader.

What we need to do is get back to basics if we want to see change in our society.   In teaching and practicing honor because that is what decides your future.

Chapter 3

THE POWER OF HONOR

Encouragement and Honor Will Increase Production

It doesn't matter what field or profession you are in – whether you are an entrepreneur, a doctor, teacher, nurse, store clerk or politicians, head of state – we all need encouragement.

Oftentimes, people want others to feel as if they are not making a difference, whether it is in your personal life, job or within the nation. Regular encouragement will refresh, renew and refocus a person to continue to do the task that you are called to do.

There are many ways to encourage and honor someone. The first thing we must each learn to do is to encourage ourselves. Problems will arise – financial, marital, economic, health or national problems, but according to I Samuel 30, we must encourage ourselves in the Lord as David did!

David was facing familial and national problems. There was distress from every direction and fear consumed the people. They were ready to stone their leaders. But David strengthened himself in God. He realized that faith was his title/deed, and his faith in Almighty God was so lifted that it removed the mountains and brought the solution for him to recover all. Further to that, it brought spoils – great financial wealth – that would help him and his entire organization and administration. Oftentimes, adversity comes to bring us back to our original focus and foundation.

There are many things we can do to encourage and honor someone on a daily basis. Each person needs it – it brings increase to your organization, your nation and to your family.

Power, gifts and resources are tools given to us to motivate someone each day; and the things that we have been through in life and have overcome, we can use it to encourage and honor someone else who needs it! Seeing your life being an impact on the lives of others and bring change gives encouragement.

Regardless of the negative things people say about you, there must be some good that you have done in your life!

Honor is a major part of encouragement. The main fact that certain blessings and wealth cannot be transferred to individuals is as a result of a lack of honor. Abraham, one of the wealthiest men in the Bible, learnt the key of honoring – he knew how important honor was as a key to access and promotion in any situation.

He honored God, the king and his own earthly father. As a result, great blessings, favor and wealth were given to him.

Exodus 20:12 reminds us that honor increases life. No nation will be able to turn until they learn to honor!

How to Encourage and Honor

Honor God by putting Him first in all things; in worship, in the giving of our tithes, offerings, time and resources! Proverbs 3:9-10 show us that honor encourages God, and God in turn encourages us through blessings, increase, wealth and prosperity.

Honor your staff and bosses through tangible rewards. I Peter 2:17 reminds us to, "Honor all men, love the brotherhood, fear God and honor the king." This means that honor brings access! Plaques, trophies and even a certificate can encourage and motivate an individual and increase production. Remember that our greatest assets are people – not hardware and software.

Additionally, employ the use of money when honoring your staff! Money will encourage a person – there is nothing wrong with money! Money is a legal tender that deals with our basic and daily needs; the lack of money can cause great distress and increase your medical expenses.

Honor your wife/husband by doing things for and with them that allow them to recognize that their value is greater to you than any material thing. Honor in your marital relationship increases its value and never depreciates!

I take this opportunity to honor God who has given us life, as well as the management and staff of the The Gleaner Company for the hard work they do to bring The Gleaner into the daily lives of its readers. Finally, I honor you, the readers of this column, for your continued support.

Honor the Leader/The Anointing

You cannot get The Anointing or certain blessings unless you place value on the Anointing of your Leaders/Mentors. Many disrespect and dishonor the Anointing on their Leaders/Mentors and pay the price. Gehazi did it! Eli's children also dishonored their father; they did not respect the anointing that was on their father! What should have been their birthright to be passed on to them was instead passed on to Samuel who was not Eli's biological son! Their actions also cost them their lives!

When you are in the midst of or have access to mighty men/women of God, don't let familiarity blind you! Familiarity is the enemy of your breakthrough! It causes you to lose sight of their spiritual authority. It causes you to see someone in the flesh and not in the spirit.

There are battles that you are going to go through, but it is going to take the Godly wisdom and the Anointing of your leader to bring deliverance to you and prevent you from going down. It is not about years of service and how long you are serving a leader but *how you honor him or her*!

If the sons of the prophets honored Elijah, God would never bypass them and raise up Elisha who was previously ploughing his father's field.

To *honor* means *"to esteem, respect, pay homage, to hold in high respect."*

Some people only honor those they feel are honorable according to their view/standards. But not so! Even if your parents are poor, they are still your parents and must be treated with honor.

Seek after what is inside of your leader – the positive attributes and principles! Ask them how you can help them to fulfill the mandate and the vision God has given them. Never allow friends family or familiarity to rob you of the great things God has in store for you by not honoring the Leader/Mentor and the Anointing placed over your soul.

Honor God And Be Rapture-Ready!

As we continue to draw closer to a new era, it is becoming more evident that it is unlike anything we have ever seen before! The year 2015 is shaping up to be a very interesting year; God is calling His people in holiness, righteousness and absolute integrity. Many over the years have been going through hardship, and this year seems as if it is the hardest anyone of us has ever been through. But now we need to ask the questions:

1. When was the last time you attended church; paid your tithes, or fasted? (Hebrews 10 v 22-25, Psalms 122.)

2. When was the last time you honored the Lord with the first fruits of your income? (Proverbs 3 v 9-10)

3. When was the last time you truly sought the Lord? (Matthew 6 v 33)

4. What have you done with the talents and gifts God has given you? Are you using those gifts to worship God or help build His house?

5. Are you in obedience, worshiping Him as you ought to and doing what you need to do according to His word in order to be blessed?, (Deuteronomy 12 and Deuteronomy 28)

6. Are you following God's instruction when He gives it to you to be blessed? (Genesis 22).

7. When was the last time you told someone about Jesus? (Matthew 28: 18 − 20)

8. Does God fit into your weekly schedule?

Now, God is calling His people to renew their minds according to Romans 12: 1 − 2 and stay rapture-ready (1 Thessalonians 5 v 1-11; 1 Thessalonians 4: 16 − 18). A time of blessing and outpouring is coming for the faithful! A time of lamentation is coming for the world and the unfaithful! A shift is already taking place; God is calling His people to be ready and to work in the vineyard for Him! (Matthew 20) and to seek Him first (Matthew 6: 33) and all will be added. Do not seek the things of the world, seek God and trust in Him.

Do what you can to gather, equip and reach the lost and dying, the abused, those who have already given up on life. And remember, Be Rapture-Ready.

Chapter 4

BE FREED

John 8: 31-32 says, *"Then Jesus said to those Jews who believed Him, "If you abide in My word, you are My disciples indeed. And you shall know the truth, and the truth shall make you free."*

We are living in world where everybody wants to be free to do whatever they want. In the recent US Elections liberals have said they at free to do whatever they want with their own bodies - abortions, sex changes etc. Many have said that they are free to live any life they choose - sexual immorality etc., and many Christians voted for that and support it.

When someone becomes a Christian, he/she then becomes free from his/her old slave master and Jesus has bought him/her back from sin. Once Jesus owns you, He becomes your Master and you become slaves to righteousness. No one can have two masters. You are either a slave to sin or a slave to righteousness.

In pursuing freedom or what freedom truly is, many lose their freedom and end up in bondage. It all started in the Garden of Eden when God gave Adam and Eve everything they could ever possibly want or need. They were free, but God gave them one instruction - do not eat of the tree of the knowledge of good and evil. That was an instruction requiring obedience. But Satan convinced them that they are not free and that they should not obey that instruction so they can be truly free. In other words, don't listen to God, do what you feel like doing and then is when you are truly free.

Their act of disobedience caused them to lose their freedom and as such, their obedience to the alternate instruction caused them to become slaves to sin.

There is no organization that does not have rules and guidelines, but the guidelines must be Scriptural/

Romans 6 specifically teaches us about being slaves to sin versus being slaves to righteousness. In Paul's response to the supposition that Grace encourages or permits sin, he uses the analogy of slavery to combat a casual attitude toward sin and issues a stern warning on the consequences of yielding to sin. A person is a slave of that to which he gives obedience or that which he recognizes as his master. If he obeys the command of sin, then sin is his master and he is moving in the direction of eternal death. If he obeys the command of righteousness, then righteousness is his master and he experiences true life. Paul encourages those who were once slaves of sin to renounce it and instead become slaves of righteousness if they want to be truly free.

Holiness leads to freedom. Sin is a slave-driving task master that demands total commitment and ultimate death. No Christian can have two bosses, hence when one becomes a Christian, we must follow what our new slave master Jesus Christ instructs us to do. We cannot be Christians while living the life of the world. (Romans 6: 22)

John 8 also teaches us that if we are truly disciples of Jesus then we must abide by the Word of God. The Word of God is what helps us to maintain our freedom. Most Christians don't read the word, so how can they truly be free? Every Christian should read John 8: 35 - 36, "*And a slave does not abide in the house forever, but a son abides forever. Therefore if the Son makes you free, you shall be free indeed.*"

The word 'son' here has nothing to do with gender - it has everything to do with your relationship with God the Father. The Jews were saying at that time that they were free because they were children of Abraham, but Jesus was saying that if you reject the Son of God, then you have no moral relationship with the Father. Likewise, many Christians say they are Christians, yet they refuse to abide by God's Word and principles - the very God they say they serve. They prefer to get the benefits of one who serves God while abiding by the instructions of the world. Party and fornicate all week - go barhopping, yoke themselves to whomever they choose, choose any shepherd they feel like on any given day, whatever they feel like doing, wherever and however and with whomever they choose - ignoring the principles of God or trying to merge His Word and Principles with the world's views and opinions of God and His Word. This cannot be so. John 8: 42 - 44 reminds us "Jesus said to them, "If God were your Father, you would love Me, for I proceeded forth and came from God; nor have I come of Myself, but He sent Me. Why do you not understand My speech? Because you are not able to listen to My word. You are of your father the devil, and the desires of your father you want to do. He was a murderer from the beginning, and does not stand in the truth, because there is no truth in him. When he speaks a lie, he speaks from his own resources, for he is a liar and the father of it."

Romans 8: 14 shows us that only those who are led by the Spirit are the sons of God. What spirit is leading you?

Romans 8: 19 -21 says, "For the earnest expectation of the creation eagerly waits for the revealing of the sons of God. For the creation was subjected to futility, not willingly, but because of Him who subjected it in hope; because the creation itself also will be delivered from the bondage of corruption into the glorious liberty of the children of God."

Many in the prophetic circle often misquote this Scripture. We cannot truly impact the earth unless we are walking in HOLINESS! We are slaves to righteousness. God owns us totally. Sons walk in obedience. Sons are free from sin. Some Christians can't even follow simple instructions. When we walk in holiness we will see the manifestation in the environment so we won't even have to point out global warming because sin affects all areas.

Truth be told, the world has the wrong concept of what freedom is and it is impeding us from truly experiencing genuine freedom - the kind that can only come from God.

I am a slave to righteousness and Jesus is my Master because He paid the ransom for me and bought me back.

We Need To Be Free

Each day we realize that many of the nation leaders around the globe seemed to have a vision for their nation – but without the people!

Jesus showed us that building the people is the most important factor in order to build nations! He took untrained, uneducated men and transformed them into world changers!

When the building of roads, a sky scraper and human sexuality become the number one vision for a nation, then there is a serious crisis. When billions are being spent to open abortion clinics, while they fail to spend it on education, then you know we have a problem. Abortion, spiritual or natural, is the number one cause of the global crisis we are now facing.

Many of the good politicians that had a vision to make significant changes never made it. They were wiped out because of Abortion.

We are now seeing a major attack on our boys as a ploy to wipe them out because of their purpose. Why not empower our boys. Many of them have within them solutions for our problems. So many speak about 'women and children – but the boys are being neglected! All that is being done is the building of more prisons.

God created man to rule and to lead. What the Political scene needs are real men with backbone to stand up and do what they have been purposed to do!

Have a Purpose

Everything God created has a purpose. You have been created with a purpose and a mind to accomplish greatness! No human mind should be wasted. Remember that no-one can fulfill your purpose for you. Your purpose is greater than going to church to warm the bench as usual! Likewise, the church's purpose is not to focus on erecting buildings as a part of the 'pretty building competition', it is to empower and build the people – that is primary! The building is a secondary issue. (Matthew 28: 18 – 20; Luke 4: 18 – 19)

When the church fails to do that, then we have all manner of "rights" groups with wrong motives rising up to deal with issue that would have been handled by the people if they had been built up and empowered.

The reason you are alive and have survived stillbirth, abortion, accidents, rape, robbery, miscarriage is to fulfill a purpose. Everything that happens to your life – good or bad – is a key to your life's purpose.

Some of the scientists, inventors, and those who are considered great men – whether or not they believed more in the Creation than in our Creator – they fulfilled a purpose God had for them. Today we are beneficiaries of their fulfilled purposes.

In days gone by, there were physical efforts by leaders at all levels to *do more* to bring positive change. Today, in light of technology, they see no need to make an effort to bring change to a nation's situation. They sit back, press buttons and push paper, and they make no move to go out physically to see and know what is happening within or to their nation unless it is "press-worthy" to do so; or for deriving personal pleasure.

The moment God created us, He put our dreams, visions and assignment as well as the path we must walk and even the people who are to be around us within and around us in order for us to be great! Now remember that the devil tries to imitate everything God does, so he puts around us the wrong people, influence you to think the wrong way, and even to marry the wrong person; and wrong decisions give rise to other wrong decisions being made.

You can't discover your purpose by working two jobs for survival. In a case like that, you will become spiritually bankrupt. Spiritual bankruptcy comes about when we fail to get into God's Presence. Whether you believe it or not, whatever you spend time with most often, you become just like that. Nations are now refusing the good things that would bring about positive changes and instead embrace and support those things that do not! All they seem to do is borrow loans as an alternative when God wants us to be debt-free. God wants us to be debt-free. When we are not debt-free, the lender dictates the terms, policies, how, where, when and what we do and can impose their own beliefs on the borrowers. When we are debt-free, we are truly free!

The Crippling Effects of Fear

One of the greatest hindrances/obstacles to advancement and progress is fear. It will stop you from walking into greater things and will paralyze those who want to try something new/better.

Many nations are ruled through fear. The rulers set up systems to intimidate the people and manipulate them into going the route the rulers choose for them – not necessarily a path that the people desire to walk. Communism is the most obvious example that would come to mind. However, it is not the only system wherein this takes place; it also happens within a democracy. Freedom of Speech for example, seems quite democratic, but can also be enforced to intimidate and shut down another's viewpoint or expression.

Fear is the biggest enemy to our faith, as it diminishes your trust in God. It hinders us from stepping out into the deep, and causes us to focus on the giants/obstacles standing before us, rather than allowing us to focus on the God Who has the answers/solutions, and Who can change any situation in an instant!

Fear always brings doubt, unbelief and prevents us from seeing the manifestation/realization of our goals/desires. For example, many times, people have dreams/visions/plans/ideas that are so big it looks impossible. But the most important thing is to take that first step toward realizing them. Fear will show you every possible obstacle and tell you how illogical, ridiculous or even how stupid and unattainable your visions/dreams/goals are; and always shows you the easy way out. Fear will show you all your limitations – age, height, size, academic qualifications (or lack thereof) and tends to show you a false picture of yourself. It shows you yourself as a grasshopper, while it displays your enemies or competitors as giants that you cannot conquer.

Fear distorts your vision and always tells you, you are not good enough! Fear robs you of your inheritance and hinders you from taking your rightful place in society. Through fear comes failure, discouragement, negative thinking, complaining, debt, death and causes you to disobey the voice of God. There are many people in the different facets of our society that can make positive, significant change(s). They also know and see a lot, but they go silent because of fear. That is why crime, violence, oppression and political correctness. Some say, "If I tell the truth I am going to lose my job!"

Fear causes you to give your enemies too much credit. Fear causes you to discern matters incorrectly and overshadows positive reports with negativity, discouragement and doubt.

However, the opposite of fear – which is FAITH – says 'we are able to overcome the mountain that stands before us! We have the power and the capacity to change, succeed and prevail!'

How do you know that you are not qualified for something, or that others are stronger than you, or that you are not able to do something, if you don't even try? Many are afraid to go back to school, to start over or start something new, simply because they are fearful. Fear always has you comparing yourself with others, and tells you that you are not qualified enough and so you put yourself in the minority as a result of the low self-esteem that it brings. What about Faith, Grace and Favor?

There are people who are afraid to embrace certain relationships because they don't think they are worthy of such relationships, they are also convinced that this is how they are seen and so they settle for less in all things.

There are many times people are in their season of change and promotion, but because of fear, they hinder the manifestation/realization from taking place. So much so that if they are given an instruction to do something by/in a particular time/season, they don't proceed, so they miss a blessing.

Fear divides and causes people to distrust their leaders and those who have the capacity to help them. It brings a person into self-pity and also directs them to follow the wrong leadership. It also blinds a person from seeing the good, and the goodness of God in a situation - even when God sends a deliverer to take them out their situation. As you advance in your promise, then fear causes obstacles to come which increases your desire to go back to where you are coming from – back into the oppression and depression.

When the Children of Israel advanced toward the Promised Land, they encountered obstacles, but fear told them it would be better to go back to the place of bondage and die there than to die on the journey to a better place.

Born To Win

The journey to better may have obstacles, but you have the capacity to overcome.

Chapter 5

THE OVERCOMER IN YOU

Not everyone is a prophet. However, everyone has the ability to prophesy or speak words that would bring change!

If God created the universe by speaking words, and we are made in His image, then we too have the capacity to speak our very future into being! Every word we speak, good or bad, will bring forth a harvest. We must decide what harvest we want.

First, God wants us to begin speaking positive words to cancel all the negative words we have spoken about ourselves or that others have spoken about us. (Proverbs 16: 23 – 24)

Confessing positive words brings healing, peace, creates light, life and builds our self-esteem. It brings hope and creates a new path for us. It brings victory!
:
Proverbs 18: 21 lets us know that a person's life largely reflects the fruit of his tongue. To speak life is to speak God's perspective on any issue of life. To declare anything negative is declaring death, and re-injects the past into your current situation.

We will be held accountable for every idle word we speak on a daily basis. The negative words we speak will determine whether we are righteous or whether we are condemned.

Many times we see people suffering and it is the result of what they speak about themselves. (Matthew 12: 36 – 37)

The tongue causes defilement, brings strife, war, sickness and curses. The Word of God even tells us that we can tame animals, but the tongue is more difficult to tame and releases poison. Many die, never recovering from this poison.

A negative or untamed tongue is controlled by a python spirit. Many churches, families and organizations break up because of the tongue. God wants us to use our tongues to create miracles and to change our environment as well as to bless our children! In the same way that fear is a spirit, faith is a spirit!

When the spies gave a negative report, based on the giants they saw in the Land of Promise, it nearly destroyed the entire camp. Your negative words can become the trap that destroys you. Jesus shows us that there is power in our tongue. He showed this to us in Mark 11, when He spoke to the fig tree to dry up from the root and it did!

There are many things and cycles against which we need to speak! There are curses that need to dry up from the root and we have the capacity to make it happen. There are contrary winds and storms that tend to come against us, but which we can speak against to stop them from coming in our direction. Within your mouth, you have the power to remove any obstacle coming against you.

(Zechariah 4: 6 – 7) We are children of Grace and we have the authority within our mouths to remove or speak against any opposition.

God wants us to find a Scripture of Promise and begin to declare it daily! (Hebrews 11: 3; Genesis 1)

Joel 3: 10 reminds us that the weak should say they are strong; and if words create the environment, we can create a Godly environment for us and our families.

Declare these words today!

I Am Blessed!
I Am Walking In Favor!
I Am Walking In Power!
I Am Walking In Victory!
I Am Approved And Access Is Granted!
I Am Brilliant!
I Will Make It!
I Am A Champion!
I Am Beloved!
I Am Beautiful/Handsome
I Am Motivated!
I Am Strong!
I Am Forgiven!
I Am Rich!
I Am A Billionaire!
I Am Prosperous!
I Am Able!

You Can Make It In Hard Times

Many are now crumbling under these hard times. Some are giving up and others are even taking their own lives! People are now realizing that politicians are not representing the interests of the people the supposedly represent, but instead their own interests! BUT, regardless of how hard it is, each person must know that they can make. It just depends on a person's daily, personal choices. Each day God creates opportunities and access to blessings. (Psalm 68: 19) The bad economy has nothing to do with one's daily survival. You can get blessed in any season. (Psalm 68: 9)

We must begin to embrace the fact that the politicians don't determine your future, you do! They are not responsible for your children's not going to school, neither are they responsible for the poor choices you may make – adulterous relationships, common-law relationships and producing children you refuse to take care of; and spreading HIV and other sexually transmitted diseases. It is a waste of precious time and much energy to become bitter with family members (particularly those overseas) who can't help you on a regular basis.

Even if you are/were a school dropout, for whatever reason, you can still rise out of your present situation. Don't blame yourself and dwell on past mistakes, think about your future and rise like a phoenix. Most of us are allowing our past to determine and even be our future. God made us with many gifts, talents and ideas to rise out of our present situation. There is always something in our midst during the hard times, to bring us out of poverty, debt and hopelessness! (2 Kings 4: 1 – 7)

Many are looking for the easy way out so they get involved in 'drug transportation', illegal weapons possession and other criminal activities. Many involved in these activities are being used by rich individuals who don't have the desire to go the straight and narrow way and don't care about who they use. Ask the question, "How many 'big men' do you see going to prison?" Even if you are fatherless, it is no excuse for getting involved in crime for survival! There are many persons who were without a father in their lives but they made it big. Persons such as Dr. Rex Nettleford, Mr. Gordon 'Butch' Stewart, The Matalons, The Issas, William 'Bill' Cosby, Dr. Benjamin 'Ben' Carson - they all started from poor backgrounds, some without fathers present, and their names are known today.

Don't Sell Yourself

You are more valuable than an iPad, Blackberry, Android or any amount of Cash! Don't allow yourself to be used sexually to get these things. Instead:

- ✓ Seek for an education! You have the capacity to own businesses and still maintain your moral values!

- ✓ Be wise! Keep away from the Brand name phenomenon. Most of these Business moguls have made it already - You can make it too! Why would

✓ you spend 3 or 4 times the money to get brand name items (especially if you are financially challenged) when you could invest that in your education or in your own family for a better tomorrow!

✓ Dress simply!

✓ Drive simply! You don't need to drive in luxury priced vehicles when you can get something less costly and save.

Don't sell yourselves to get rich. Some of the greatest things you can have are good health, a solid education, a debt-free home and a family. One of life's greatest rewards is having the ability to help humanity!

Back To Basics

In hard times, for survival, it is cheaper and healthier to make use of the things that God has placed in our surroundings or environment. For example, it is cheaper and healthier to drink lime and water or the basic lemonade than it is to guzzle processed drinks. Limes and lemons have 10 times the health benefits of the processed drinks and 'juices'.

It is healthier and less expensive to grill or bake your meats than it is to microwave the processed foods. Not only does it damage your health, but it pushes up your electricity bill significantly. The good old wood or coal fires are better for our health. I am sure that there is someone who can come up with good ideas to make that work despite today's fast-paced global existence. Where there is natural spring water, cut down on importing water and source your own! Boil and purify your water and stop spending so much on imports!

Finally, when God gives you dreams and visions, it is to help you to be a better person. Stop gambling your life away! Find some people less fortunate than yourself and give what you were planning to gamble and see what a difference it will make to them and for you.

Simple Keys to Overcome Life Struggles

1. Trust God not man, politicians, welfare or job.

2. Believe that whatever God has promised you will come to pass.

3. Make vows to the Lord and honor them.

4. Pray and ask God for His *grace* and *favor* daily.

5. Always pray according to Mark 11, asking God to move your obstacles.

6. Always sow seed/give donation – for example, to feed the poor.

7. Volunteer –in your church, community or child's school.

8. Maintain a forgiving heart.

9. Seek the Lord for Him to send you good Godly mentors/mentorship

10. Control and discipline your tongue. Stay away from gossip, negative people and unedifying conversations.

11. Keep away from the spirit of ingratitude. Honor/be a blessing to those who have helped you to grow and succeed.

12. Always give Thanksgiving to God.

Overcome Fear by Faith

Fear is a spirit that Satan releases to defeat us. Fear breaks down our defenses. Satan will give us visions of sickness, failure, disaster and other adversity including death to bring fear upon us to back down or away from our God-given vision. Fear is the opposite of Faith! Faith is our victory!

Faith is what allows us to climb over and overcome obstacles and hindrances. Hebrews 11:6 says Faith is what pleases God. Righteousness comes through faith. (See Romans 3:21-26, Romans 1:16-17). A true revelation from God comes through faith.

The moment you start to walk in the realm of faith, you will start to receive victory. Remember the opposite of faith is fear. Fear will start to attack you as soon as you are close to a breakthrough; but faith is what destroys fear.

Remember *fear* is a spirit. When you confess and declare the word of God. It will cancel that spirit that is released on you. Fear must not be taken lightly, it is a dangerous spirit. This is the spirit that brings spiritual and natural abortion. It cancels the prophetic word. Remember it was fear that allowed the ten Hebrew spies that Moses sent to spy out the promise land in Numbers 13 and Numbers 14 to see death and defeat all over. But Joshua and Caleb walked in faith. They saw victory, prosperity all over.

Also, the woman to whom the prophet Elijah to 1 Kings 17 was sent was gripped by fear. The only things she saw were fear, death, defeat and gloom. To her, it was all over. But when the prophet Elijah spoke the words of faith, and because of her obedience, everything changed from death and defeat to prosperity in the midst of famine.

You may be facing a situation that you may be bankrupt soon or any other critical situation that seem threatening. Fear may be speaking to you in your dream or visions in the night, but once you obey the instructions I give you, and move in faith, fear will be defeated.

It does not matter what the enemy is telling you; what matters is what God is saying.

It does not matter what you are going through; or how high your mountain looks; or how powerful the enemy seems to be. In Numbers 13:29-30, the promise land was reported by the 10 fearful spies that "the Amalekites live in the Negev; the Hittites, Jebusites and Amorites live in the hill country; and the Canaanites live near the sea and along the Jordan". Then Caleb silenced the people before

Moses and said, "We should go up and take possession of the land, for we can certainly do it."

It doesn't matter what kind of "-ites" dwell in the mountain. The mountain is where God wants to bless you. The place where you are positioned is where the enemy will want to dwell. But God said "Fear Not!" Caleb said to the people in Numbers 13:30, "Let us go up at once and take possession for we are well able to overcome it". God said, "… It is time for you to go up above your obstacle."

The word "able" means to have power, having the capacity to prevail or succeed. It also translates to "Can", "could" or "prevail". It is therefore time for us, to go up and take our possession, our inheritance and walk in the Promised Land.

When Fear starts to speak to you, it means something big is about to happen.

Prayer to Attack the Spirit of Fear

Follow these instructions:

1. Anoint your head daily with oil (Olive Oil that has been blessed and declared to be the blood of Jesus)

2. While praying place you hand over your head

3. Use the blood (the blood of Jesus) daily over your head. This means to declare coverage of the blood of Jesus.

4. Repeat the following prayer

Father in the name of Jesus Christ, we come to you right now. Your words said in 2 Corinthians 10: 3 - 5, "For though we live in the world, we do not wage war as the world does. The weapons we fight with are not the weapons of the world. On the contrary, they have divine power to demolish strongholds. We demolish arguments and every pretension that sets itself up against the knowledge of God, and we take captive every thought to make it obedient to Christ."

We command fear to be broken from our minds. We declare faith to be increased now in Jesus Name. Possess all our promises. We bind ancestral spirits, spirit guides, familiar spirits, infirmities, afflictions, death and Hades, and we cover ourselves with the blood of Jesus. We defeat every spirit that the enemy release upon us to defeat us. We bind mind-blinding spirits. We bind the spirit of Fear, and we release faith and miracles now.

As in Isaiah 35: 3 - 7 "Strengthen the feeble hands, steady the knees that give way; say to those with fearful hearts, " "Be strong, do not fear; your God will come, He will come with vengeance; with divine retribution He will come to save you." Then will the eyes of the blind be opened and the ears of the deaf unstopped. Then will the lame leap like a deer, and the mute tongue shout for joy. Water will gush forth in the wilderness and streams in the desert. The burning sand will become a pool, the thirsty ground bubbling springs. In the haunts where jackals once lay, grass and reeds and papyrus will grow."

We receive the blessing in 2 Timothy 1:7, which says that "… God has not given us the spirit of fear but a spirit of power, of love and a sound mind". We have the power of God, the perfect love of God, through His Holy Spirit. We have the mind of Christ according to Romans 5:1-5, which state – "Therefore, since we have been justified through faith, we have peace with God through our Lord Jesus Christ, through whom we have gained access by faith into this grace in which we now stand. And we rejoice in the hope of the glory of God. Not only so, but we also rejoice in our sufferings, because we know that suffering produces perseverance; perseverance, character; and character, hope. And hope does not disappoint us, because God has poured out His love into our hearts by the Holy Spirit, whom he has given us".

We thank you Lord for victory and deliverance over the spirit of fear in Jesus' Name. Amen.

Are You a Grasshopper or a Giant Killer

"For as he thinks in his heart, so is he…" Proverbs 23: 7a

We cannot have success until we begin to see ourselves as God sees us. Many times, we tend to forfeit our purpose, because we often see ourselves as grasshoppers rather than giant killers! Fear can cause us to paint a negative picture of ourselves. It allows us to compare ourselves with others and come up with negative results. For example, when the children of Israel were given the land they started to describe themselves as grasshoppers, comparing themselves with the giants. They even convinced themselves that this is how the enemy saw them.

How do you see yourself? Do you consider yourself a failure, a loser, broken or insignificant? How do you think God sees you? You would be surprised! *You are a giant-killer*! How do you think the enemy sees you?

The main fact that the enemy is influencing you to see yourself in a negative light, is an indication that the enemy fears you and sees you as a potential giant-killer.

It is not about what those around you think of you. The important thing is that it is about what God thinks about you!

You will never leave where you are until you decide who you are. Stop looking at where you are and at your past or present circumstances. Start looking at where and who you should be. If you see yourself as a grasshopper, you will indeed become a grasshopper. If you see yourself as a giant-killer, then you will be a giant-killer.

You have to see yourself by faith what you want to be before the manifestation come. By creating a positive picture, you are allowing the manifestation of the unseen to be seen. Don't for one minute think that because you don't see something it does not exist. In that case the wind does not exist!

Never focus on what you lack, focus on what you got! What you've got can create far more than what you lack. In 2 Kings 5, the woman was focusing on her lack while she was ignoring what she had. The little oil she had could bring her out of debt and create a massive breakthrough! Never focus on your lack more than what you've got! Begin to take stock – do an inventory.

A person may not qualify for much when they apply for a particular job or office, however there are gifts and talents they possess that can create greater wealth than what they were pursuing in the first place.

A grasshopper mentality thinks about their past hurts, past failures, past mistakes and is overwhelmed with fear which stops them from moving forward! They are like politicians who are always speaking about their past achievements or what the opposition did in the past. When we begin to speak about our past more than our present or future, then our future becomes our past and then we will see the same cycles over and over in our lives. Could it be that politicians focus on their past successes and the oppositions' past failures to keep people from recognizing the present nonsense in which they engage?

Regardless of what evil has be done to you, the only way that they will be a part of your future is if you allow yourself to be consumed by bitterness and un-forgiveness. The enemy cannot be a part of your future unless you bring them into it. It's not worth it to allow your thoughts to dwell on your enemy!

The reason we can't even break the back of crime is that there is greater focus on the obstacle rather than the opportunity. Grasshoppers focus on the obstacles and hindrances.   Giant-killers turn their obstacles and hindrances into opportunities for promotion.

When crimes rates increase, more gated communities are built.   There is more security and unnecessary walls are erected.

Begin to focus on the 'land' – your victories! Stop focusing on your past relationships, those failed relationships it will blind you from seeing your bright future! There are many in the Bible! God saw Jeremiah as a Prophet to nations, but he saw himself as a youth who was not as qualified as other prophets. Moses saw himself as ineloquent. Gideon – a deliverer; God saw him as a mighty man of valor. He saw himself as the least. So the moment we push past our negative thoughts on how we see ourselves, then we will walk into God's purpose for us.

There are many problems globally which await the solution within you! You are a GIANT KILLER!

Destroying Your Goliath

Each day we come against many battles. There are battles we fight that would get us weary and discouraged – especially battles that seem too big for us – a Goliath! Each of us has a Goliath that we must conquer and defeat if we are to move forward. When Goliath rises, there is always an opportunity for promotion.

Your Goliath is anything that stands before you and your purpose or promotion. It is always something huge which you cannot destroy through your flesh or natural abilities.

Can you imagine that you are broke going up against a politician who is wealthy and has all the support and the capacity to bribe and buy whomever they choose. That is a Goliath!

A Goliath can be situation you are up against that is beyond your limitations to resolve. Just think of a small army of 300 with very little resources, up against an army of 3 million with all the resources they want. That big army – that's a Goliath!

You may have a lawsuit against the elite of the society, and you are unknown who has no connections. You may be in sports and you are up against a mighty team with all the resources and you have very little resources with which to compete. Within your mind you are going to compete, but you don't believe that you can win. Think of someone facing bankruptcy or foreclosure, having no one to turn to and having no money or defense to fight. Maybe there is sickness or a serious struggle that could only be resolved. These examples of issues that could be called your Goliath.

When we are facing giants, we are always considered the underdog; but for those who are risk-takers, they know that the underdogs always carry greater value and pay higher dividends. No one will ever believe that the underdog is a serious contender or that they can get victory! Never focus on the size of your Goliath, because that is when the fear factor will show up and tell you that you don't have a chance so don't even try! Fear cause you to focus on the natural; faith allows you to focus on the spiritual!

Facing and Fighting Your Fears

Faith in Jesus Christ destroys fear! When facing and fighting your fears or the product of your fears, you *must* let the Holy Spirit be your Guide. Furthermore, our weapons must be Prayer, Fasting, Praise, Worship, Thanksgiving and Giving. We must pray for the enemies' defeat. We are going to fight and win regardless of the size of the enemies' resources!

Many times people will cry and ask why they have to have a Goliath at all. But to be honest, without facing a Goliath, there would not be any access or reward/benefit to take you to the next place of growth. There would be no David without a Goliath – he was unknown before there was a Goliath.

Facing our Goliaths bring out the hidden talents and potential in us. Furthermore, we cannot apply human logic to address it; neither can we employ the same methods the enemy uses. Witchcraft is not an option! All we need to do is seek the Lord for tactics, strategies and direction. (Psalm 25) Always remember that God is greater than Dagon; so obedience to God is key for victory when facing your Goliath.

Remember, we cannot defeat what we refuse to confront; because what you refuse to confront will defeat you.

Pray this prayer daily to defeat Goliath according to 1 Samuel 17: 45 – 47.

Father, in the name Jesus, I come to you right now, to confront and conquer my Goliath in areas of relationships, lawsuits, sickness, injustice, sabotage, bankruptcy, delay, denial, crime, violence fear, witchcraft, plots, traps, sabotage, financial problems, competition, corruption and personal insecurities.

This day (_today's date_) the Lord will deliver you into my hands. In accordance with 1 Samuel 17: 45 – 47, I declare "You come to me with a sword, with a spear, and with a javelin. But I come to you in the name of the Lord of hosts, the God of the armies of Israel, whom you have defied. This day the Lord will deliver you into my hand, and I will strike you and take your head from you. And this day I will give the carcasses of the camp of the Philistines to the birds of the air and the wild beasts of the earth, that all the earth may know that there is a God in Israel. Then all this assembly shall know that the Lord does not save with sword and spear; for the battle is the Lord's, and He will give you into our hands." In Jesus' name I pray. Amen.

When You Feel Like Giving Up

Regardless of everyone's status, the struggles of life affects everyone, and there are times you will feel like giving up. Sometimes you feel so discouraged that you don't have the strength to try anymore.

Problems come in many ways – sometimes it is a lack of opportunities, sickness, hardship, no employment. A person may even be highly qualified but can't even find food to eat. Each time they try to get an interview, they end up disappointed and feel unsuccessful.

Sometimes you pray and it seems as if your situation is getting worse. Meanwhile, there may be an inner voice saying "It doesn't make sense, give up." The main fact that you are alive despite the struggles, means you are still in the game. The temptation may come for you to indulge in certain activities to get a job, or keep a job, but you know deep down that you must not do it, simply because it is wrong.

When you are discouraged and feel like giving up, it is a distraction, and that is the time one of your greatest blessings is about to come into your life. Even when your situation seems dead to the point that it stinks, know that there is always a time for resurrection. God is able to roll away the stone, remove the grave clothes and cause you to come alive! God can remove the bondage from your feet. Some may be sabotaged, but God is able to roll away your stone and set you up for a mighty comeback! Never forget the power of persistence in prayer. Our problems, at times, exist to help us to develop spiritual muscles, and so that all the glory will be given to Him for your breakthrough. There are many in this season who are discouraged, but this is a distraction for you not to focus on the bigger picture. Distraction blinds us from seeing what God wants us to see. It could be a revelation that will bring you into billions of dollars – the next invention, solutions for governance and leadership.

We are in the greatest time, where the Babylonian/Secular system is no longer relevant and cannot work in this era. Sometimes the hardships we go through is to change our mindsets.

Jesus outlines in Matthew 6 that worry brings stress, anxiety and pressure. If God can take care of the birds of the air and other animals, what can't He do for you?

When a woman is close to giving birth she goes through a time of anxiety and a myriad of emotions. Then comes the prize! So birthing comes with pain, but then there come the blessings.

Failure

Failure is not your stop sign, but your greenlight for greater things. Failure is a set up for success.

There are many people that some considered to be failures. Read about Mr. Walt Disney - he was a newspaper editor that was fired for having a lack of creativity. Today, Walt Disney's company is in 7 locations throughout the world on 4 continents and employs over 62,000 people with over 44,000 visitors per day in their Lake Buena Vista (Florida) location alone.

Sir Winston Churchill's successes came through several failures. His famous quote said – "Never give in--never, never, never, never, in nothing great or small, large or petty, never give in except to convictions of honor and good sense. Never yield to force; never yield to the apparently overwhelming might of the enemy."

In your time of struggle, you will find your best gifts coming out. You know your greatest friend. It brings the greatest creativity out of you. Speak positive things on a daily basis within your environment. Surround yourself with positive people of faith. Your present circumstances don't determine your future.

The emotional battle is real, but if God did it for others, He will do it for you! If He brought you out before, He will do it again. Every great person came through failure and fire.

If you are experiencing a lack of success in your life or if others are telling you that you are a failure or not creative enough, then that is your indication of the untapped greatness that is yet to come out of you. Keep going!

Chapter 6

REJECT REJECTION AND RISE

Throughout the Bible there are many instances where we see the least become the greatest and the weak becoming the strong! Those who were considered to be the least and the weakest are the rejects of the society/marketplace! They are the ones God always raises up to bring both solutions and glory in hard and dark times.

In II Kings 7, the entire city – indeed a nation – was enduring hard times to the point of cannibalism, and it was the four (4) rejects that God used to bring victory and blessing to the nation of people.

A nation was constantly suffering defeat, and it was David – the reject, that God used to defeat the Philistines.

A people with no hope – and it was One Who came and was rejected by His own yet He made the ultimately sacrifice for all, so that we would not need to suffer such a death nor experience it ourselves.

When we look at our own music industry, it is refreshing to see the rise of a 'Mr. Gully Bop'. As long as he remains clean with his music and pure in motives, he has the potential to rally the rejects and anyone else who feels like things are over.

For 2015, many rejects will come to the forefront and bring hope and solutions to the people. We are inspired by those in the Bible such as Gideon, Joseph and Esther.

The society has been failing because the wrong persons have been placed in positions. That is why we will need leaders who can see things the way God wants us to see things.
There is nothing wrong with intellect, but intellect without God's spirit becomes ineffective. Man looks at the outward appearance or circumstance – age, titles and even educational achievements for example; but God searches the heart – He looks beyond all that to the core of an individual.

As a nation, we have failed to capitalize on many opportunities throughout 2014, because we have refused to seek God concerning His will as it relates to all things great and small.

The problems we are now encountering is the ignoring of God's guidance by leaders. There is a focus now on the New Age doctrine and the 'religion' of Secularism leading us on a path of chaos!

1 Corinthians 1 says that ". . . the foolishness of God is wiser than men . . ." God uses the base things, the rejected things, despised things, the weak things – according to the eyes and minds of men – and confound those who deem themselves wise – and bring about miraculous things! So all those who ridicule the weak, the rejected, the despised, the poor and even the Word and the things of God, they are about to get a rude awakening!

God always uses what is considered as nothing to bring to naught what is thought of as great.

So regardless of how highly a politician esteems him/herself, they can bring no change for the better unless they become the beneficiaries of God's wisdom and guidance, as well as His grace and favor!

I encourage every organization and every political party to begin to look again within their organization and find those they consider to be unusable and begin to use them. Don't be like the West Indies Cricket Management Team who keep looking at the wrong areas instead of the Administration and its practices. Nobody who truly enjoys cricket wants to see the West Indies Cricket Team demoted from Test Status. Mr. Cameron, I hope you will take heed.

Family

Many have failed to put the family on the forefront in the past. We better begin to do that as the New Year approaches. Passing laws which will negatively affect the family will create more problems! The family is the first line of government and that foundational mechanism must be fixed. So, Common Law relationships need to be addressed seriously from every angle if we want to see economic change. Fixing the family will reduce crime. Many times we blame the police for things we should be addressing. Many turn to crime because there is no true Justice System. The justice system does not truly address the issues for the poor.

It was Haile Selassie said, "Throughout history, it has been the inaction of those who could have acted; the indifference of those who should have known better; the silence of the voice of justice when it mattered most; that has made it possible for evil to triumph."

Rejection Hinders True Potential

Rejection starts from the womb. It is one of the greatest hindrances to the true potential to individuals and ultimately to nations.

Simply put, 'rejection' means 'to refuse to accept, acknowledge, use, believe; to throw out as useless or worthless; discard; to rebuff (a person).'

Many mothers, during pregnancy, experienced rejection in many forms, which became so much a part of them – their mindset and as a result was ultimately passed on to the child; either during pregnancy or at birth. Some women were abandoned or abused during pregnancy, raped and became pregnant.

Psalms 139: 14, Luke 1: 44 and Jeremiah 1: 5 shows us that when the child is in the womb, in fact from the moment of conception, they have a spiritual identity. As a result, hearing, feeling, smelling, emotions, thought patterns are developed during pregnancy and even their assignments are 'downloaded' during this time! They can hear sounds, they respond to the emotions of their mothers and to the voices of their fathers!

So what happens during pregnancy to the mother directly affects the child she carries and it is embedded in the development of the child.

When a woman becomes pregnant and is rejected by the father of the child she carries, double damage takes place! The mother becomes fearful, disappointed, bitter, desperate, and feels betrayed and alone. This culmination of negative emotions becomes the root of rejection that both mother and child.

Sometimes rejection comes from mother to child when the child is the exact image of his/her father who abused or rejected the mother. Further to that, rejection increases when the father rejects the child and deems the child a jacket while he fully embraces other children. Then it is further increased when that same child attempts to reach out to that father for love, affection and acceptance, and is ignored – rejected! So it becomes an issue throughout their entire life and the cycle continues.

Rejection damages the soul and no medication can fix it! However, Psalms 23: 3 tells us of the healing that is there for the soul – ". . . He restoreth my soul . . .", and it is when the soul is healed that true peace and prosperity will come.

Negative Words

Negative words contribute greatly to rejection. Proverbs 18: 21 says, "Death and life are in the power of the tongue . . ." Words stick and often carry through to adulthood. Some persons would say that it is better if you hit them than curse them. So when, for example, influential persons in a child's life – parents, teachers, other adults – call the children dunce, fat, ugly or worthless, and then declare prison and death on their own children it carries through with them unless it is broken.

Clearly if we are going to deal with crime, we need to understand rejection.

VIP's And Politicians

Many of our public officials suffer from rejection. The nation cannot be truly healed until they are healed. Some of them have never been told by any one that they are loved. Some never had the love of a father expressed to them and their trust has been betrayed. That is why some of them play so tough and cold – they hide behind a mask.

A person who suffers from rejection will always be defensive, have low self-esteem and untrusting. Such persons don't allow anyone to get close to them.

Rejection is a stronghold, and behind every stronghold is a form of bondage. Behind every lie there is a fear. Behind every fear there is an idol. Until we deal with root of rejection, your true potential for greatness will be hindered.

Rejection says, "You are not good enough", "you are not attractive", "you are not eloquent", "you don't belong in this category", "no one loves you", "no one cares for you", "you will never make it."

It's time to shut that nonsense down! It is time to recognize and accept that you are fearfully and wonderfully made! You are great and you are going places – you are the head! You are smart, intelligent! **Walk In Victory!**

Rise! Take Up Your Bed and Walk!

Now more than ever, many are stressed, depressed and discouraged. Fear is gripping many and even more are giving up hope, especially small business owners. Each and everyone needs to know that discouragement is a factor that causes one to get weak, distracted and lose one's zeal.

When someone gets discouraged, it is usually when he/she believes that they have tried everything within his/power and the expectation has not been met. A person may be praying for a breakthrough, and yet things seem to become worse rather than better. Some become discouraged because they may not get the respect they think they deserve. Another may become discouraged when they think their work is not appreciated and they are ineffective in touching the lives of others. Discouragement can also be caused by delay, denial and betrayal. These are weapons the enemy uses to get us to become discouraged or depressed. This leads to self-pity and then many will want to give up because they may then see themselves losers or failures. Some will even begin to question past decisions and doubt their capacity to make the right choices - whether in business, jobs, marriage and life itself!

Discouragement saps your energy and blurs your vision. Always remember, nothing remains the same. Every problem has an expiration date! Whatever discourages you is only temporary. Whatever losses you experience, you have the capacity to bounce back.

Always remember the story in John 5, which speaks to us individually and as a nation, that regardless of the condition we are in, we have the ability to rise, pick up our beds and walk.

You will never walk unless you rise first; and that first takes place in our minds. You have to see yourself standing up before you truly do!

People who lie in bed are either weak, sick or asleep. If we want change, then we have to change our minds! Those who rise are always alive, awake or well. In this story, we see a great multitude who were either impotent, blind, paralyzed and/or withered. They all became helpless and hopeless. Many of them were looking for movement in the water – which symbolically is a spiritual revival.

However, even as the stir came, the man was unable to step in to be made whole. He was there for 38 years! His excuse was that he was looking for someone to physically put him in the water. His problem was his dependence on man for change and not on God! In the same way we look to politicians, international monetary or funding agencies or other grants to pull us out of poverty. When we depend on many to save us, we will get discouraged and depressed.

Each time this man sat at the pool waiting and the water was stirred, someone else stepped past him and stepped in themselves. This is what has happened to Jamaica and the Western countries; they have shifted their focus from God and have become paralyzed. In this instance, the problem with this man was his mindset – his way of thinking and looking at things.

Wholeness will only come when we rise up out of that way of thinking. When one rises, one's thinking begins to change; strength and power will come.

Interestingly, after he rose up he didn't even need to step into the water, he took up his bed and walked! Before, he couldn't even stand up; but now he could pick up the bed he used to lie on and walk with it!

If we think we cannot do without borrowing, then we will never stop borrowing!

If we think there is no other way except loans, grants and sale of assets in order to rise above a situation, then we will be paralyzed.

If we believe that there can never be a third party in the nation – whether USA, Jamaica or any other such nation – then we are denying true leaders and game changers from coming forth; and we will always be wandering in political instability.

If we think that a foreigner, a man or a woman is our savior, then our condition will become worse.

If we truly desire change, then the time has come to rise up out of traditions, rituals, religiosities, logic, double-mindedness, oppression, immorality, pride and witchcraft!

Chapter 7

NEVER GIVE UP ON YOUR DREAMS

We have often heard of the praises being sung of the success of prominent men and women locally and globally; but not many spend time to listen to the struggles, suffering and obstacles they went through before they experienced/achieved success. Never be jealous of or envy a person's success, because you don't know what they have gone through to be where they are today.

God has given each of us visions and dreams. Have faith in God and never let go of the vision that God has given you. You *will* make it to the top one day!

Each person is unique in their own way. One of the problems that can hinder us is that in life, we tend to focus on other people's success and use it to measure ourselves and that is a direct path to envy and jealousy. In life, people will always have an opinion of us and what we do and even how we do what we do. So for example, if you are poor, you will get poor treatment; and if you are rich, you will be treated as such. But don't allow the treatment you receive to cause you to become bitter and unforgiving. When God gives you a great vision/great dream, you are going to experience great struggles too. Many may ask the question, "why and I struggling so much? Or "why am I experiencing battle after battle?" But recognize, that there comes a time when you will value the struggles you have been through, because those struggles gave you great wisdom, experience and strength.

God may allow us to walk a path – a tough path – because He wants, that when we come through, then we can extend mercy and compassion to them as they grow likewise. For example, you would not know how to treat someone going through financial crisis if you have never been through it before. The same thing applies with illness and injustice. We live in a world where many in influential positions have not been through anything much, as a result they make poor choices, or make decisions for the field from a desk.

A person becomes a better manager/leader when they have been through some things. So while you reach for your dreams, don't give up during the struggles. Recognize that if you have never been through certain things – struggles, challenges, obstacles, then you may very well become an obstacle to others. There are pastors who preach about faith, for example, but they have never truly had to walk or live by faith. Many of them live in a church manse, and earn a salary with benefits, but they don't know how half of the congregation lives or survives.

Remember this and be encouraged, your struggles and suffering are the tools of preparation for the great wealth transfer and the shift that is coming. Never forget Joseph or Esther in the Bible. Their hardships and times of poverty prepared them for kingship and kingly places.

Always remind yourself, you are born for a purpose. The earth is always turning and a new day is coming. Every problem has an expiration date. Hold on to your dreams and don't quit! You are a champion and God is preparing you to soar like an eagle. You don't have to turn to a life of crime or prostitution. We can use the life story of the NBA Champion Kevin Durant as an example. At eight (8) years old he told his mother he would be a champion. He suffered many things – sleeping on the floor, being raised by a single mother (father absent), no food or clothes at times and was even criticized by journalists that he would not reach anywhere in the NBA! He is a champion today! Lesson: NEVER QUIT!

So hold on to your dreams. The Get-Rich-Quick mentality will get your poor even quicker. When failure comes, learn from it and keep moving. Always surround yourself with people who have been through and have overcome. There times you have to move away from negative people. Jesus had to lead a man out of his community before He could heal him.

Champions never stay down when they are knocked down, they keep getting up and they continue to fight! Never stop confessing/declaring your dreams. Mentally paint a picture of yourself succeeding. We are born to win. Losers are those who refuse to fight. Use your obstacles and failures as a ladder for promotion. Man may forget you, but God never does. When there is no enemy, there is no promotion or reward. Without the giant, David would never be king.

Don't dwell in the past, look to the future!

The Future Is Bright

Many are going through rough times – hardships, financial lack, sickness, job loss, economic strife and hopelessness. Even some men and women of faith are giving up because to them it seems there is no future. Remember, however, that what you are going through is only for a season! Everything changes except God and His principles. Time changes, seasons change, friends change, people change, regimes change and laws change.

Your present circumstances don't determine or dictate your future – regardless of what you are going through. The instructions you follow and the choices you make (Deuteronomy 28) can change your circumstances in an instant! Who your mentors are, and those to whom you listen can help you to walk into a bright future. Naomi was broke, but because of her integrity and her wisdom, Ruth was ushered into millionaire status.

The term 'future' means 'a time to come; what is to happen; prospects yet to come or be, or have not yet taken place.' The future is always greater than the past. You cannot change the past, but you can change the future! Remember this, your future is not in past things, your future is yet to come. The positive words that we speak can create a positive future! (Proverbs 18: 22) The things of the past are already done! What say you of the future?

Politicians are guilty of this, continually pointing out past failures of other and declaring it over the future of the country if their opponents should rise to power. As a result they create a cycle of spoken failures just waiting to manifest in the future!

Isaiah 42: 9 "Behold, the former things have come to pass, and new things I declare; before they spring forth I tell you of them."

We all need to stop dwelling on the past, and stop trying to bring past things into the future. Anytime you find that those in positions of power or leadership are bringing up and dwelling on the past failures of others, particularly their competitors or opposition, it means that these people have no good or clear plans for the future.

Despite all that, Jeremiah 29: 11 – 14 reassures us that God has a plan for peace, prosperity, deliverance and healing. He promises to answer prayer.

Walk Boldly Into Your Future

What is past, present and future to us is already past for God! He is the Omniscient God and according to His Word, He is the Beginning and the End! It means He already knows the end!

Many have already lost hope in the political and financial systems globally! There is refusal to change while the poor continues to suffer and die under the oppression! But do not worry! The future is bright! In due time, God will raise up leaders who will not walk the path of their forefathers; leaders who will have a new vision, a new platform, new ideas and who will not be afraid to bow their knee and submit to God's instructions. (1 Samuel 17: 38 – 39)

Keys for a Bright Future

Order   when you increase order in your life you will increase peace, growth and productivity

Obedience   it brings, change, promotion, blessing and increase.

Plan   make a list of the things you desire to have for the future such as debt write-offs, debt-free home, debt-free business, speak it every day and watch it come to pass.

Wisdom   Seek for Godly wisdom, which will allow you to make the right choices for the future.

Willingness To Change   Your location can also determine your future God has a desired and specific place where He chooses to bless you. (Genesis 12: 1, Genesis 22, Deuteronomy 12, 1 Kings 17)

Mentorship   Whomever you see as your mentor and advisor will determine your future decision-making

Remember that the obstacles and hindrances you encountered was a preparation for the future. Sometimes persons are shifted from you – whether for a season or a lifetime – so that you can embrace the bright future that is ahead of you!

Chapter 8

YOU WERE BORN FOR A PURPOSE

God created us all with gifts, talents and solutions to change the world. It is critical for us to bring it forth. But in bringing it forth, many are afraid to start small, when we are told not to forsake or despise small beginnings. Fulfilling God's purpose is the only way we will experience real joy.

Oftentimes people confuse happiness and joy, but they are two different experiences. Happiness is momentary and external. We can be happy and still not experience joy. Joy is lasting and reaches a deeper place within us. It is an internal fruit and only the Holy Spirit can allow you to experience joy because it comes as a result of being in God's will.

Many may have billions and be happy about it, but still have no joy, because they are not fulfilling God's purpose on their lives.

There are many today who feel that their career/chosen path is their purpose, but not so. For the most part there are many whose career path has nothing to do with their purpose – the things that God has created you to do. Their purpose is not being fulfilled and that is why they are unhappy, lack joy and are struggling today. Many die never fulfilling what God created them to do, because oftentimes they were more interested in pursuing material gain.

There is a cure, vision, revelation or solution within your DNA to come forth to help mankind. Every person that has been born in this world was born for a purpose. They were born with specific instructions embedded within them. Each is unique, special and your life is valuable. You were born to make a difference.

You Don't Decide Your Purpose

God is the one who decides your purpose! He is the one who places you in the geographical location He wants you to be in order to fulfill your assignment. When you resist your purpose, painful things occur in your life. That is why we ought to be against abortion; because our purpose is decided before we are conceived. Jeremiah 1 specifically states it. Whether we believe in the existence of God or not does not change that.

Discovering and Fulfilling Your Purpose

Have you ever felt incomplete? Have you ever felt unhappy regardless of what you have accomplished? Have you been feeling restless recently and are getting dreams and visions, some of which you don't understand? What are the things that make you happy? What makes you sad? What are the things that burden or hurt you? Have you ever asked yourself these questions –

- ✓ "Am I in the wrong field/career?"
- ✓ "What is my purpose in life?"
- ✓ "Why am I going through the things I go through in life?"

All these are clues to help you identify your purpose and to stir you into action.

Why do you seem to hate injustice more passionately than the other person? Maybe your calling is Law! Why does it hurt you more deeply than the next person, when someone you don't even know has been badly hurt, abused or killed? It could be that your calling is an Advocate or a Health Professional! Maybe you have a vehement passion against the corruption or the economic problems and suffering you see occurring daily and others around you think you are going overboard with your passionate discussions? It could be that your calling is in the Political arena or in Economic Policy Making!

Maybe you are just going to work for a salary/pay, but there is no joy in what you are doing. Maybe you are one of those who just watches the clock. Some of you have had near death experiences and suffer many things - disappointment, extreme adversities, abuse and even things you don't tell anyone but by yourselves you cry. Many of you have tried to fit in with the boys or girls but it doesn't work. You are different!

When God created you, He put greatness within you, so you have to be set apart. You are an eagle and an eagle does not sit with chickens. That is why you feel odd and incomplete. Even when someone have retired, and there is still a fire burning within you, then it means that there is still more within you and you have not yet fulfilled your purpose!

Each person was created to solve a problem. Many times when we see chaos, economic problems, injustice, crises with our children – those things come about because the one who was created to deal with that problem is not in proper position. Each time we pray or cry out to God to bring change to an organization or a nation, the answer always lies within a human vessel. That is why Jesus Christ always focused on building the vessel first. God created the earth and equipped it with all He created in it before, then He placed mankind in it. Likewise, He created us – the human vessels – and has equipped us with the solutions within us for the problems that we would encounter.

Within each person is embedded instructions to carry out and when they fail to carry out their assignment, many lives and many things are at stake. Your education is not your purpose, and for many, your job is not your purpose. Some of the clues to your purpose include – the things that make you angry when they happen but bring you great joy when they are addressed or fixed; the things that grieve you.

When you see disorder in the society, for example, how do you feel about it? Do you become extremely angry? If so, it is an indication that you are a born leader. Leadership is a gift given by God. (Romans 8: 7; Romans 12: 7 – 8) Likewise, teaching is a God-given gift! So this is why there are so many problems within the education system and schools in general. Some of the wrong people are in the classrooms.

Value Your Life and Fulfill Your Purpose

Regardless of the circumstances that exist, we must remember to do two of the most important things we can do in this life. 1) Value your life 2) Fulfill your purpose.

Many want to give up hope now, and to many it seems as if darkness is overcoming light and hopelessness and joblessness are taking the lead. But, one of the reasons that this is happening is that people are fulfilling their purpose.

We must recognize that we are each unique and are created to solve problems. When we refuse to walk in our purpose, then we lose and we are denying the world of the solutions that we were created to solve.

Step Over The Hindrances

One of the greatest obstacles and hindrances in our lives are often ourselves! Faith without works is dead! Don't just criticize and talk for the sake of talking. Do something constructive and make this world a better place. Utilize the gifts that God has given you, as well as the resources, and touch someone's life. You can be a mentor to someone. Help an abandoned child! Show love to someone's child! The cemetery is filled with unfulfilled purposes and unexpressed ideas.

Begin to cut down on waste – and start with your household first! Cut down on entertainment, use of electricity, wasting food, gambling, use of alcohol, and even the A/C in the car. Use some the savings to help the less fortunate. We must lead by example. By doing this, we are demonstrating the love of God! The Word of God says that when we give to the poor, we lend to the Lord, and the Lord is looking for lenders!

Start the Pursuit

It is not your mind telling you to start that business, or to go back to school or to register your company; it is God pushing and encouraging you to bring out what He placed within you. Don't allow fear, fear of failure, obstacles or the criticisms of to hinder you from bringing out what God has put in you. Everything starts with a seed – you have to start from somewhere.

By principle, everything in life - much like a tree – starts with a seed. You plant it, cover it with the soil, you water it, watch it, fight even the elements for it and it begins to shoot up as a tender/delicate plant. You begin to believe in it. Recognize that in life, betrayal, disappointment and discouragement will come. At times you may even feel so discouraged and as if you are not making a difference and you may even think you should give up on that vision because it seems dead. Some people will even tell you that you missed it and you should try something else. But what you didn't know is that the seed you planted was taking deep root in the ground. God was using your struggle to allow you to become stronger and wiser. God was using your challenges to develop you into a great tree. A great tree is about to come forth from the small seed. The seed/plant goes through infancy, youth, prime, senior, twilight - much like you and I. One day you are going to get up and see the change in effect – that the small seed brought major expansion.

There may be people at different stages – some at the infancy stage, youth or twilight – not in age but in process of fulfilling your purpose. So it is time to monitor the tree's base, check for foundational problems, trim the tree and allow the tree to bear.

From great tests come great vision. Always remember that a tree goes through different stages, so don't give up on your vision. Keep ploughing and fighting, you have to first believe in your vision before others can believe in your product.

A time is coming that the loan they refused to give you and the help that you asked for and didn't get, are the best things to happen to you, because when you reap the success, then no one but God can get the glory for it.

A person is never too old to start fulfilling his/her purpose. When you are fulfilling your purpose, it's more than just accomplishing a task – you are actually saving lives.

Add Value to Lives

Every decision we make must be tied to the value of life! So let your goals and objectives for the future include some of the following:

✓ Edify someone each day

✓ Take the time to be in the Presence of God each day. He needs relationships, not one night stands. This is where you will find/receive the solutions, healing and how to make better choices

✓ Evaluate your stewardship and see where the pitfalls are, so that you can be a better person/leader

✓ Sow good seed on a daily basis – quality time, talents, and so on, knowing that you reap the harvest of whatever seed you sow

✓ Maintain a forgiving heart – let no bitterness dwell in you

✓ Ensure that whatever plans you have, God is a part of those plans

✓ Be thankful and appreciate those around you

You are born for a purpose – so fulfill your purpose.

There are some people in different nations, whether we like them or not, regardless of our political affiliation, or personal preference there is greatness within them and if they fulfill their purpose, great change can come. Here are a few examples

Barry 'Barry G' Gordon, well-known Jamaican radio personality, has the ability to bring revival within the nation among the Youth. He is a prophet from His mother's womb.

Former Senior Superintendent of Police (Jamaica) James Forbes, has a Pastoral calling. He can bring change to the inner city and within the Police Force. He should read Matthew 6 and John 3. God must be his only source. If he should fulfill his purpose, great turnaround will take place.

Gordon 'Butch' Stewart, internationally known, Jamaican hotelier and businessman, has the solution for a business revolution. If he should focus on fulfilling his purpose, things would unveil within him that he never knew was there.

Former Prime Minister of Jamaica, The Honorable O. Bruce Golding, his work is not over yet. There are solutions within him to bring change politically and economically.

Paula Llewellyn, CD QC – Director of Public Prosecution (DPP), has gifts in her to mentor, motivate, teach and counsel. She can do great things to help the abused girls.

Fae Ellington, OD – internationally-known Jamaican actress and media personality, has a gift to bring back order particularly to the state of women within the nation.

Beverley Anderson-Duncan, media personality and has great revelation within her to bring change within the nation.

Former Jamaican Parliamentarian the Honorable K. D. Knight has a gift to establish proper governance and human rights.

The Honorable Peter Phillips – Jamaican Government Minister, has the gift of Administration and Pastoral calling.

Marion 'Lady Saw' Hall, former dancehall artiste, has a gift to help the abused.

Rexton 'Shabba Ranks' Gordon, internationally known dancehall artiste, has a gift for community transformation.

Former Jamaican Police Commissioner Owen Ellington – his gifts address politics, youth and community. He would be a good Youth Minister.

Marcia Griffiths, OD – internationally known Jamaican Reggae artiste (formerly of Bob Marley and the Wailers) has a gift to mentor and counsel and she has the gift of compassion.

President Barak Obama – has a gift to teach and for outreach

Imagine if each person begins to fulfill his/her purpose, what major changes would take place.

Chapter 9

KNOW THE SCOPE OF YOUR CALLING

Many times in the business arena and in the Church, leadership will get frustrated, and companies and churches struggle at times because they are unable to service those within. Until you identify who you are called to and where your greatest support lies, who supports your business/church you will not move forward.

Luke 4: 18 - 19, says, "*The Spirit of the Lord is upon Me, because He has anointed Me to preach the gospel to the poor; He has sent Me to heal the brokenhearted, to proclaim liberty to the captives and recovery of sight to the blind, To set at liberty those who are oppressed; To proclaim the acceptable year of the Lord.*"

My calling is to the poor in spirit, poor in finance, to set the captives free and to bring healing to the brokenhearted and recovery of sight to those who are blind spiritually and physically. So if you are a prostitute, if you messed up, if you are a misfit, if you are rejected, or if you are a sinner or you are unrighteous - WELCOME! I am not called to righteous people, nor religious people, nor to those who have already arrived.

Paul was called to the Gentiles so God gave him the grace to deal with the Gentiles. He was set apart (Romans 1: 1 - 7) Many leaders - whether business or church - are spending too much time focusing on the wrong areas. Some even get disheartened and discouraged when certain people within the society don't accept them. You will not be accepted by everyone in the society it is not Scriptural.

The Pharisees did not accept Jesus, and neither did His own city/town. When God gives you an assignment, keep going, keep doing good! Give hope to people! Stop moping and groping and focusing on those who criticize you and reject you.

Do an analysis and see who your biggest supporters are and focus on them; those who genuinely help you.

Who are your biggest clients?
Who always supports your work no matter what?

Those who are called to you will follow and support you. Recognize that you are not called to everybody.

Organizations fall when they change their mandate. Many companies are going into markets and territories that pull them away from what makes them great. Recognize that while businesses must be willing to take risks, they also need to draw the line between taking risks and shifting from the vision. What if KFC decided to open a supermarket chain; or if Digicel, AT&T or Duke Energy started selling Life Insurance?

Acknowledge and embrace your difference and run with it. Many churches are diverting from the mandate - even transforming to attract a certain set of people; or doing things which are not Scriptural. Now the many churches are becoming a laughing stock. Jesus did not try to fit in at all. Stick to your mandate despite the challenges. Know your clientele know your sheep. Many times the poor are more appreciative of the work you do and the sacrifices made and they need your difference.

Embrace Your Difference

Many Pastors today say they are called to the rich, but the rich don't truly need God until they become poor. Some of these church leaders today want to emulate Dr. Phil or Steve Harvey or John Maxwell – they simply need to be themselves. Many politicians are trying to be like President Barack Obama. One thing about President Trump – whether he was loved or hated, he never tried to be like anybody else, he was himself – take it or leave it.

Quite a few Women of God try to be like or sound like Prophetess Juanita Bynum, but all they need to be is themselves.

Don't try to change your personality. Only those who know their difference and the scope of persons to whom they are called. David was a misfit. Several tried to change him even his mode of dress to keep him within tradition, but He did not fit in it. If he did not take of the traditional and just be himself, he would not have survived Goliath. Always remember this, your difference is there to deal with what is to come, not for what already exists.

Have you ever heard each time something goes wrong that the only solution that can come is to pass a law to make something work. So the only solution we can find to any issue is to *'pass a law'*. Passing a law may not be the best solution at all times. It may even bring greater oppression. Interestingly, while they are passing these laws, they are not passing laws to hold themselves accountable.

Chapter 10

KEYS TO SUCCESS

We are in a critical season in which God desires individuals, nations and businesses, as well as ministries and marriages. However, many are being held up due to unpaid vows.

Many have walked away from their vows. Many have made vows with God for fame, power, riches, jobs, marriages, children, and even to get healing. They made vows that they would feed the poor, work for the Lord and other humanitarian efforts. However, to date, they have not done what they have promised the Lord. Some have made vows with men and women of God stating that if they received certain blessings they would in turn bless them. But, upon receiving the blessings, they don't pay their vows.

It is a sin to make a vow without paying it. There are consequences to breaking a vow Job 22: 27 Psalms 50: 14, Psalms 56: 12 and Psalms 61: 8.

Vows bring great blessings. However, when we fail to pay our vows it brings great consequences. Even nations are now being shaken because of the vows that their forefathers made with God and the persons in charge today have forsaken these vows. God honors and defends all vows. He never forgets vows. Vows tie you to your blessings and prosperity.

A vow is a covenant with God or man. It is a contracted agreement that can either be verbal or written which can be made with either God or man. People make vows for protection, provision, the presence of God, peace, victory and for guidance. People also make vows to abstain from sex, alcohol, drugs and even food, in order to be successful or to gain power. (Genesis 28: 17 – 22; Numbers 21: 1 – 3)

Every vow carries conditions and consequences. Vows have allowed impossible situations to become possible. Pregnancies for example, people have made vows in order to become pregnant. (1 Samuel 1: 11). We have even seen people who were robbed of their inheritance make vows and became established as heads of nations. The least became the most important within a nation because of the vows they made unto God! (Judges 11: 29 – 40)

Many have failed to pay their vows after receiving breakthrough either because it is difficult for them or they have forgotten. But God does not forget!

We have seen vows save lives and in fact, many have arisen from their sick beds because of vows. Many have been taken out of debt and bankruptcy because of the vows they have made unto God!

Many have become millionaires because of the vows they have made. (Genesis 28: 20 – 22)

Vows create miracles and changes lives for good! They authorize God to give you the blessing in advance.

Many gain promotion through the vows they have made. Some have even said, "Lord I know I'm not qualified, but if you could give me that position, I will serve you." Some have even vowed to help the poor. Some say that they would even help the poor if God did something for them. Still others have said, "God if you heal me I will put God first and give to the children."

Many people are now struggling and it seems as if everything is falling apart. They are losing access in certain environments and they no longer have the favor they did before.

If something is not going right in your life or your organization, you need to think, carefully about your vows and find out if there is a vow you forget to pay. A vow is a promise and can also be used as a promissory note. Many times it is a vow that saved us from adversity. Great businessmen, Prime Ministers, Sports and Entertainment personnel, Church leaders, will let you know that it is the vows that they made and it made them so successful today. For many made vows to God to be where they are. Many have been healed of sickness and diseases, rescued from bankruptcy and other disasters, will tell you that the turnaround happened because of a vow that they made.

Pay your vows and walk in this season of prosperity.

Hardship: A Qualifier for Success

Everyone wants to succeed and prosper! But not many are willing to qualify for that success! Hardship is the number one criteria.

You may, for example, be told by your bank or financial institution when you are going through hard times, to write a Hardship Letter indicating the measure of difficulty you are having which hinders you from meeting your monthly, financial obligations! Don't be ashamed to do so, because the hardship you are enduring is maturing, processing and will ultimately promote you. Each time you go through hardship, you come out wiser, brighter and better!

It is not wise to follow a leader, in any area, who has not been through hardship. Hardship increases your wisdom, knowledge and understanding as well as your faith in God. The best resume one can possess, is what they have been through and overcome.

There are many people who will speak on issues, and have been placed in authority within an organization or a nation, but the question is, 'Do they have the necessary experience that will help them to do the job right?' How about this! 'Do the pastors, bosses, bankers and financial leaders know what it is to go to bed hungry and not know where the next meal is coming from?' 'Do the bankers know what it is when you need to make a payroll and not have any money at all to do so, and no overdraft facility?' 'Have business and national leaders ever had to look at their children and tell them it is not their turn to eat today?' If you have been through any of these situations, or any truly difficult circumstance, then greatness is coming out of you!

Hardship gives you a testimony, and it can be used as a weapon that will demoralize and defeat your enemy. (Revelation 12: 11) Also, each time you come out of hardship, that experience makes you richer and wealthier spiritually, and gives you greater insight, ideas and solutions.

Hardship and the Mind

Hardship renews your mindset. Each of our mindsets must be renewed on a daily basis. There are different mindsets that hinder you from walking into greatness and realizing your true potential!

These are the mindsets that are hindering the growth, change and reformation within a nation.

- ✓ *Logical Mind*
- ✓ *Analytical Mind*
- ✓ *Political Mind*
- ✓ *Religious Mind*

You cannot analyze or reason faith! The reason individuals and nations are not getting the change they require is that how they think remains the same at all times. So, before your circumstances, environment and situation change, your mindset must change!

One of the reasons God allows some persons to go through hardship is that He wants their way of thinking and their views to change.

Some people would never change or even lobby for a positive change to take place if they didn't go through it themselves! (There are some interesting times ahead!) Hardship opens your eyes to view others differently. For example, have you ever known of anyone who would fight people tooth and nail for a position or promotion, but as soon as hardship reaches them, their very actions and heart change?

Hardship is not an indication of failure, but of the coming success! Don't be mistaken, hardship can also be as a result of disobedience. Nevertheless, hardship can be one of the best trainers you can have.

You may be going through hardship and it feels like everything is being stripped from you on the outside, but God is doing a greater work and you have been increasing on the inside! You are better qualified, wiser, stronger and on your way to greater!

Faith in God Brings Success

We are living in a time of great challenges and economic constraints. Some people are experiencing hopelessness, joblessness, and there is even an increase in suicides and suicidal tendencies. Despite all these problems, each of us has a hidden force within us, the capacity for faith in God that can bring success into our lives.

What Is Faith

According to the Oxford dictionary, *"faith"* is *"a complete trust or confidence in someone or something."*

Faith, is believing in God without doubt. Believe in God that what you desire or pursue will come to pass. Faith is your heavenly currency/heavenly money.

The world would be a better place today if we put our complete trust/confidence in God to achieve our desires/goals. Many leaders today, put their faith in bailouts from donors such the IMF. Some have faith in military might; for some it is their advisers and PR mechanisms; for some it is the voodoo or witch doctor; others have more faith in gambling than even tithing. Many leaders are failing because they no longer put their faith in God for success.

If we exercise our faith we can change our circumstances. We can change the direction of our beliefs, our lives. We can change the state of our bank accounts (Mark 9:23) God requires all of us to have a 'NOW-faith', (Hebrews 11) which can advance our expected goals and objectives by 10 years or more.

To exercise our faith, first establish what your needs are. What dreams, desires, goals, or objectives would you like to achieve? Do you need a job? A car? Healing? A miracle? All of these can be achieved through faith in God. What change do you want in your life? Are you tired of hopelessness? Through faith we can see the manifestation of His works.

Faith in God can turn a country that is on a path of gloom and destruction onto a path of prosperity! When the difficulties of life face us, faith in God will always create a way out, in ways you could not even imagine! In facing difficult tasks, many leaders and individuals will make hasty, hard choices and follow-up with statements like, "There is no other way!" But it is a sin not to have faith in God. (Romans 14:22-23) Faith is the master key to open all doors and unlock the treasure that one desires.

Many large corporations today can tell us that when they began, it was just by faith. Through faith they have expanded and experienced growth. Even the preparation of budgets for sales projections in an organization, is faith in action. When one has faith in God nothing is impossible!

There are many things people will say is impossible. How about closing a business deal, without having the criteria for success? Let's say you want to get into business but don't have the startup funds, but because you pursue it by faith, success is achieved. So faith extends favor.

Many organizations will draw up plans for construction without having the funding to do so. This is faith in action. The very act of completing a plan without investors is really an act of faith. Many of you have great ideas but don't have the funds to make it a reality. What are you waiting for? Exercise your faith and you will see the manifestation of the evidence of things not seen. Realize that fear, doubt, logic all of those oppose faith.

Many unemployed persons will sit at home in a pity party, saying that people don't want to employ them. Sometimes it pays to get dressed in your best clothes and volunteer in organizations by faith and see what will happen. Send out resumes to organizations for positions you are not even academically qualified for, or fields you did not study! Remember faith without works is dead.

How about starting your own consulting company? Speak positively by faith daily. Words create, shape and form. Confess that you are broke, and indeed, you will always be broke! But if you confess that you are the next millionaire by faith it will happen and believe it; and pursue what you believe, you will have it! (Matthew 7:7-12)

How about getting your check book and declaring money in your account by faith? How about filling out MoneyGram or Western Union forms by faith to receive money? All strange to you, but it is faith in action!

How about symbolically getting a blank 'house key' to represent by faith the keys to your new house? Or how about purchasing a tie, by faith, for whomever your husband will be? Then as you hold strong to your faith and continue to follow His Divine principles - watch the manifestation!

When your faith increases, your wealth increases. Faith brings expansion and it can birth each of your God-given visions. As your read and share this article watch manifestation of your faith.

Thankfulness the Key to Success

We are living in a society today where people are becoming more and more unthankful. Some even say that God hasn't done anything for them. But there are so many things we should be thankful for on a daily basis and so many things for which to thank God.

For example, of the thousands of sperm to race toward the egg, the one that created you was the one that made it! Furthermore, with the millions of abortions that have taken place worldwide, you are not among that number. Thanks be to God!

Be thankful that while many of us are not faithful to even acknowledge God by attending a place of worship (of Him), He still grants us the gift of life! Even our women are free to drive a vehicle of their choice as long as they are able to get it; they are free to dress in any way they choose – in some countries it is a crime or will warrant the death penalty.

Even in this age of social media, many of us are able to access it and flaunt all our business in full public view. In some countries it is death penalty to access such modern conveniences.

In the West, many rebel and walk away from a Church if they are introduced to a dress code! In some regions, women are so covered that only their eyes can be seen. If nothing else be thankful for the region in which you live here in the West!

Thank God that we can have as many children as we choose. In some regions they are barely allowed to have one.

In our region we can own land and even pass it on to our children. In other regions, none are allowed to own land.

Thankfulness to God and man are keys to prosperity and success. Ingratitude will bring shame and demotion. Be careful how you treat your Pastor, Mentor, Employer (Organization), or anyone who has done anything for your whether great or small. Never bite the hand that feeds you.

"And one of them, when he saw that he was healed, returned, and with a loud voice glorified God, and fell down on his face at His feet, giving Him thanks. And he was a Samaritan. So Jesus answered and said, "Were there not ten cleansed? But where are the nine? Were there not any found who returned to give glory to God except this foreigner?" And He said to him, "Arise, go your way. Your faith has made you well." (Luke 17: 11 – 19)

Ingratitude stops the blessings of God on a nation, individual or organization. It is contagious. Many long-standing organizations and individuals have now fallen because of ingratitude.

Interestingly, some people only come to you when they need something. They often only remember you when they run into problems and need your help to get out! Some forget you completely when they are comfortable and have all the financial resources and they only remember you when everything has crashed and they are broke!

Never hang around unthankful people – it is contagious and will corrupt your environment. The mainstay of an unthankful person is to criticize, complain and divide! In fact, the favor and presence of God always leaves unthankful people.

For thankful people, increase and multiplication always comes upon them. Begin to thank God for your spouse, your children – because when you were without a spouse or child, you were the one crying out to God for both! Now you complain and criticize everything! If that is true, you have become unthankful and ungrateful and that is in fact a sin.

"For men will be lovers of themselves, lovers of money, boasters, proud, blasphemers, disobedient to parents, unthankful, unholy, unloving, unforgiving, slanderers, without self-control, brutal, despisers of good, traitors, headstrong, haughty, lovers of pleasure rather than lovers of God, having a form of godliness but denying its power. And from such people turn away!" 2 Timothy 3: 2 – 5

Note that the unthankful is in the same group as blasphemer and sexual immorality and so on.

Show thankfulness to God and those that have helped you along the way by reaching out to them and to someone to help them. Thanksgiving and gratitude bring great blessings and will take you to the top.

Chapter 11

SUCCESS IN SPORTS

The Sports Sector in any nation is one of the most lucrative businesses and has the potential for even greater success! It unites cultures, brings enemies face to face, and pulls together every other sector including media, manufacturing, telecommunications and even the political sector. To most it brings relaxation, enjoyment and even entertainment to masses! To others the losses in competitions bring disappointment – because nobody wants to lose. The recently concluded World Cup Cricket series brought disappointment to many West Indian cricket enthusiasts. All in all, however, sporting is far-reaching and powerful.

The questions, however, are after having success in sports over a period of time, how do we maintain the success of those involved? What do we do when continuous failure is taking place? Do we blame the players at all times or do we look at the entire organization to see what went wrong?

The West Indian cricket organization is one such structure that all other sporting organizations should use as an example.

We must recognize that when an organization that has always done well begins to slip in success, then there is a foundational problem. It means that something went wrong in the past that has cracked the foundation. It also means that there needs to be healing at every level before success can come. With regard to sports – changing coaches, selection committees and manager and players without dealing with the problem will only cause things to worsen.

For example, unfair treatment of individuals, un-forgiveness, unholy covenants, unethical business practices, prejudice (bias), will crack the foundation of an organization.

Every sporting organization must recognize that motivation is the key to success! When a player is going through a rough season, how do we treat that player, do we 'throw them away' or do we offer counsel? When decisions are being made by management, do they take the families of the players into consideration? Can we expect a player to give 100% when they are in fear of failure and removal? Do the managers/coaches possess the father-figure persona to motivate the players to the point of success, or are they only motivated by the money they can make on the players?

So it begs the question, what kind of leadership or approach is needed to recover and maintain the success of the teams within the Sports sector when they have hit a bad patch? Are we destroying or motivating the talent?

Solutions for Success

- ✓ There must be clear guidelines for new members/staff to follow so that players will not be fearful that they may be the next one going. It shouldn't be based solely on performance.

✓ All sports personnel must remember that lifestyle determines success or failure; that is, holiness (2 Corinthians 6: 16 – 18; 2 Corinthians 7: 1; Hebrews 12: 1)

✓ Ensure that you Tithe! Giving to foundations and other organization and ignoring the act of tithing, denies you of certain protection; such as maintaining contracts and financial stability. (Malachi 3: 8 – 12)

✓ Players and staff must guard against Pride. Ensure that you listen to your mentor. Follow the instructions of your security personnel. Before a press release of any kind, ensure that you seek permission before giving an interview or releasing any information.

✓ Ensure that the Team has a good chaplain that can pray and give sound spiritual guidance and counsel.

✓ Remember, your talent and successes were given by God. (Deuteronomy 8: 18) Honor Him daily.

✓ Have regular socials that include family members and give accolades to the winners and tokens of appreciation to those who lose. The losers today may be the winners tomorrow.

- ✓ Have a support team for injured personnel to help them get back on track.

- ✓ Have a system in place that players will be given platform to give suggestions that will enhance the organization in general without fear of retaliation.

The time has come for all of us to 'rally around' the West Indies Cricket Team and all sports personnel in Jamaica and the Caribbean.

We may be deemed as small, but 'we big abroad'!

Does God Have a Place in Sports

In sports, everybody wants to be a winner! There are numerous victories, defeats and all the emotions that go along with and surround the sporting arena. In addition to this, there are

Everyone who is involved in sporting activities, form the sponsors to the coaches to the fans want to know that they or the players and athletes they support will win. But it is important for all involved in sports

Isaiah 48: 17 says, **"Thus says the Lord, your Redeemer, the Holy One of Israel: 'I am the Lord your God, Who teaches you to profit, Who leads you by the way you should go.'"**

This clearly shows us that apply biblical principles in sports will bring tremendous profit in every capacity. We cannot leave God out of sports. In addition to that God empowered each player, each athlete with the equipment (body), He gave each one the tools with which to formulate the tactics and strategies – the formations, plays, and speed with which to function. Furthermore, He gives the insight and intelligence to achieve great things.

Many times various persons are selected to join or head the delegations and management teams that work with the various players/athletes. You will even see yoga specialists, health and fitness gurus and doctors, but what is not seen is a Spirit-filled chaplain.

Spiritual Strategies

Some things as simple as Fasting and Prayer can give you great victory. A 21-day Fast releases tactics and strategies. 3-day Fasts release favor against a difficult opponents. Hearing from God is the key to victory and will allow you to choose the right team.

Picking a team goes beyond talent and performance; but those who are more focused and favorable will win.

We have seen many persons who have applied God's principles and have been successful – Shelly-Ann Frazer-Pryce, Tim Tebow and Jeremy Lin. Even the Ravens who brought on the upset in the Superbowl 2013 were inspired by Psalms 91.

For the Jamaica Reggae Boyz to achieve victory and maintain it, they must continually be inspired.

Solutions

During the tenure of Rene Simoes in Jamaican Soccer history, he was inspired with the word "Jesus Saves!" Now, we need an inspiring tag line for the Jamaican Soccer team – for example – "With God all things are possible!" They also need to Fast at least 2 weeks before the match, divide the team into 2 groups to pray and seek the Lord. They also need to shift the players around.

There needs to be one-on-one sessions on a daily basis with the players to deal with their daily mindset. More player-input along with the tactics and strategies which the team should apply not just to rely on the manager or court

For the team to gel and become a cohesive unit, they need to go on cohesive unit so that bonding can take place. Talent and money cannot be the motivating factors in team selection. There must be a genuine love for the sport and the country. Efforts must be made to promote loyalty to the team, the goals and visions of the team and to the country for which they play.

In order to get greater commitment from them and a greater love among them, apply a different strategy; encourage them to interact with and play against high school teams, prep school teams, and little known clubs. This will keep stirring a fire within them and it will serve to sharpen their skills, and give them to opportunity not only to be mentors to an upcoming generation, but will also renew their focus and allow them to identify future team members.

The lifestyle of each and every player is important. 1 Corinthians 9: 24 – 27 and Hebrews 12: 1 reminds us.

Finally, equal emphasis must be given to the Netball players and other girls' teams.   They are equally important and should not be neglected.

Chapter 12

IT'S ALL IN THE MIND

The mind is the most powerful area of man and it is the area God works on the most. How we view things and how we understand them are very important. The mind also works with and influences our purpose and how we go about fulfilling it.

Ephesians 4: 11 states, "And He Himself gave some to be apostles, some prophets, some evangelists, and some pastors and teachers,"

It is important for us to recognize that the various Spiritual gifts lend themselves to different points of view, understanding and interpretation. In Numbers 15: 14, God outlines that the difference between failure and success is how we view things. So while some may see giants in an area, others may see the fruits of the land in that area. Your mindset affects your faith. For example, some people are analytical or logical in their thinking so everything has to follow that path.

1 Corinthians 2: 14 – 16 speaks about the:

- ✓ Spiritual man
- ✓ Natural man
- ✓ Carnal man

Spiritual Man

The spiritual man is far superior in his mind than the natural man. Only the Spiritual man is capable of proper judgement in issues that are:

- ✓ Judicial
- ✓ Economic
- ✓ Security (Crime and Violence)
- ✓ Sexual and,
- ✓ Political

A Spiritual person who has accepted Jesus and Lord and Savior, must have the mind of Christ. What is means is that the mandate, motives, intentions, wisdom and message must be the same as that of Christ. The Spiritual man must see things as Christ sees them. With this mind, God's people should be way ahead of the world in terms of wisdom, knowledge and solutions. No man can come to the knowledge of God with the normal way of learning. For example, many unsaved persons will quote scriptures and tell you what they think about the scripture. However, their opinions of what the scripture means is often inaccurate and their understanding is flawed. So impartation of the deep things can only come through a revelation from the Holy Spirit – hence the scripture "Deep calls unto deep at the noise of Your waterfalls..." (Psalm 42: 7a)

The Holy Spirit is the only One qualified to give us the revelation of Who God is. He is a member of the Godhead and He deals directly with man. The Holy Spirit reveals the different aspects and dimensions of God. So for you to go higher in God, you must first go deeper in the Holy Spirit.

Many who have great wealth and riches have gotten it through the spirit of the world, which brings them into darkness (the secular and natural way) and thus into enslavement.

Natural Man

The natural man does not receive the things of the spirit of God. They are foolishness to him. For example, Biblical Economics would be foolishness to the natural man; so would:

- ✓ Tithing
- ✓ Fasting
- ✓ Healing
- ✓ Repentance or Prayer for Economic change
- ✓ How sin affects the environment and the economy
- ✓ The Cross and the Blood of Jesus
- ✓ Using the Word of God to deal with crime and violence

The natural man has a lack of understanding, because man in his fallen state (functioning based on what he sees and embracing sin) cannot understand the things of the Spirit.

Carnal Man

Simply put, the *carnal man* is regenerated (is redeemed, restored to Christ), but is still living much like an un-regenerated individual. He is a believer with childish ways – being immature; living a surface-level life, and living more on human opinion than for Jesus Christ and is without Spiritual depth.

There are parts of the human mind that have not yet been challenged or utilized. There are new ideas and solutions that God wants to give to each of us. God wants man to walk in the full potential for which he was created.

The Spirit of God brings life, light, truth, knowledge, wisdom, power and authority. A person does not have to sell his/her birthright in order to get anything.

Breaking Through the Negative Mindset

2 Corinthians 10: 4 – 5 says, "For the weapons of our warfare are not carnal but mighty in God for pulling down strongholds, casting down arguments and every high thing that exalts itself against the knowledge of God, bringing every thought into captivity to the obedience of Christ. . ."

It is critical for us all to take note that on a daily basis we go through various, personal battlefields that oftentimes have the potential to either hinder us or propel us forward. If we don't overcome the negative mindsets and imaginations are part of these daily battles, then we will be hindered both physically and spiritually. Our goal then should be to overcome and break through the negative mindset.

There is a constant battle for the control of our minds; and the negative forces desire to keep us in a place of continued limitation. So each time a person tries to push forward, these forces are determined to push him/her back.

These forces that are determined to limit and confine you, and cause you to believe a lie about yourself that you are incapable of success or that you will not achieve at certain levels are called 'strongholds'!

A person having a fear of failure is an example of a stronghold. Some fear they will never lose weight; others may believe that they will never get past where their current state. Still others believe that they will never make it and that they are wasting their time; and some believe that God will never come through for them. Some women believe they will never get married! Some feel that they are not physically attractive and that no one will be interested in them. They feel that when someone tells them how good they look they are being lied to! These are strongholds!

The major difference between success and failure is the **mindset**.

It's about how you see yourself, not about how others see you or what they say about you! You must have a vision of how you see yourself, and create an idea of where you want to see yourself in 5 or 10 years.

The number one criterion for poverty eradication is a renewed mindset. If someone does not see him/her self out of poverty, then they will not come out of poverty!

A person cannot use his/her present circumstances or geographical environment to determine their future. Regardless of the amount of money a person may pump into eradicating poverty, if their minds are not renewed and they don't overcome strongholds, then they will always remain the same.

You must first see yourself as wealthy or as a graduate, or as a success – whatever the goal is – and then focus and move toward it! Ignore any negative imaginations and anything contrary to those goals; but be sure to listen for and follow Divine direction.

Recognize that negative imaginations, or anything that goes against the knowledge of God, and anything not in line with the Word of God are all strongholds.

The difference between developed (First World) countries and developing (Third World) countries is the mindset! Beyond the general ruthlessness that may exist in certain developed countries, the determination, positive work ethic, approach and focused mindset, sets those two categories apart. The developed countries will find a way to turn garbage into gold. The developing countries will sit atop the garbage and complain. The developed countries will take the waste of the developing countries, turn it into something the developing countries can use and then sell it back to them counties!

Political Strongholds

It is the perception in many countries that third Parties in countries that have only 2 Political parties, exist only to split the votes for the major Parties. They also believe that the third party will never become a contender. That is a stronghold! Such negative beliefs tend to keep one in bondage and can limit one from advancing – individually or as a nation.

A negative mindset allows a person to focus on the problems rather than seeking to find a solution. It was not the giants that hindered the Children of Israel, it was their own negative mindset and the stronghold of fear!

It is important to recognize that a negative mindset has nothing to do with one's academic qualifications.

Every individual and every nation must now seek to break free from the negative mindset that hinders our growth and development.

New Mind, New Wine New Business

To deal with the economic crises and other global social issues we are facing, as leaders we must always dig deeper each day in the things of God, in order to get the necessary solutions. Time changes, people change, the market demands change – *everything changes*! Even the rate of the dollar changes! Very shortly, you will see a shortage of foreign exchange in circulation.

Now, if everything changes, but our minds/mindsets don't change, how will we deal with the changes in demand. The old order cannot deal with the new order. The mind must be renewed each day that we may be able to accurately discern market in order to prevent loss and further problems in the economy.

The solutions that nations have been carrying out include:

- ✓ Redundancy Exercises
- ✓ Increasing Taxes
- ✓ Capitalizing on Immorality
- ✓ Giving waivers to foreign investors
- ✓ Divesting the land and assets of the nation
- ✓ Borrowing from International Lenders
- ✓ Making Decision that affect mainly the small businesses and the poor

All these decisions are nothing new and it will only create greater hardship for new businesses, new jobs, new ideas; we must embrace New Wine! It is time for us to try unconventional methods. How about this? The mind of the individual must grow before economy can grow. There is no way locally or globally, we can build on 2 foundations.

At this juncture, we don't need any more statistics, research and documentation. We need action and results!

We need to ask some pertinent questions.

- ✓ Who controls the economy?
- ✓ Who decides success or failure?

In the same way that hurdling poverty begins in the mind, likewise economic change must first start in the mind. So, before that changes, the mind must change, when the mind changes, the speech will change and when that changes, the environment will change and then our pockets will have more than change!

Without a mind change, regardless of the program we put in place, it is going to fail and put us into further debt.

How Do We Change the Mind

Before the mind of the people change, the minds of the leaders in every sector and category must change! Changes come through the Word of God, Prayer, Disaster and Adversity! Furthermore, we must look to the One Who controls change. (Psalms 121).

Did the Economic Model ascribed to our nation fit the needs of the nation and the time?

Are the programs implemented in our schools fit for the needs of the nation's children and the direction that the nation is headed?

If the mind does not change, rest assured, the sight cannot change.

We must remember a vision is also a function of the heart, not just the eyes, and all nations need a blueprint for economic change, in other words, they need a vision. If the mind is not renewed, how will we truly identify the value that exists within our nation, and catch hold of the vision which is to bring the nation out of its current state and into a place of prosperity and success. What do other countries see existing in our nation that we are not seeing? The old way of learning will not solve the mystery. Neither will we be able to discern what the priorities.

If our minds are not changed, then:

- ✓ What will happen in the next 5 years regarding job creation?

- ✓ In this present economic climate, how will governments collect taxes and at what expense?

- ✓ What will happen to University Students who can no longer afford the education; and even when they graduate, who will employ them?

- ✓ What will happen in the political arena when politicians employ the same strategies, and methods in a changing world?

"The Old Model Is Broken, We Need To Create A New One" – Ban Ki-Moon, Secretary General of the UN

"'Worldwide, more than 400 million new jobs will be needed over the next decade. That means that policy-makers must get

serious, now, about generating decent employment," said Secretary-General Ban Ki-moon at the high-level thematic debate on The State of the World Economy and Finance and its Impact on Development, held on 17 May. "It is time to recognize that human capital and natural capital are every bit as important as financial capital," he added.'

We need Vision, lest we perish!

The World Needs A Mind Change

When over 700 migrants – human beings – have perished at sea and the world is silent; when hundreds of thousands of Christians – people – have been butchered and slaughtered and the world is silent; when children worldwide are being raped, abused and are starving – left to die, and the world is silent; when a nation of people, because of famine, are subject to eating cats and dogs and the world lies silent; and then issues about human sexuality gets world focus over those issues, and the shooting of 1 ape, though a living creature – but one without a soul – is killed and there is a public outcry; something is wrong with that and the world needs a mind change!

Even Christians get caught up in the world's way of thinking! Some get caught up on political bandwagon! Even the pending U.S. Elections with front runners Hilary Clinton and Donald Trump, many are talking about a greater evil versus a lesser evil. Many are saying that if Donald Trump wins it is the end of the world. But God can allow anyone to win. Many believe that one or the other is better or the lesser evil, but there are quite a few from the past who many thought would be better but they ultimately deceived the masses! Maybe the nations need some Pharaoh's because despite all, the Church always prospers under Pharaoh!

God does not want the faith of His people to be in the wisdom of men! It must instead be in the power of God!

There are too many people with logical mindsets utilizing their oratorical skills, psychology and philosophies and even their positions of authority and their rule and works have come to naught! Some of them are trying to access the knowledge and wisdom of God by bypassing the proper channel – Jesus Christ! Their languages are now confused as it was at the Tower of Babel (Genesis 11). We can only access the things of God by a Revelation through the Holy Spirit or by the appropriate spiritual response by a man.

I recently read the articles about the crabs that have come up on Jamaican and Californian shores – which many found very alarming. Many said that this is a sign of disaster ahead. Yet one scientist from Jamaica stated that what these people were saying was utter nonsense. Such arrogance is what is messing up the world and the mindsets of others. God speaks to us in many ways and it is a proven fact that animals and insects, through their instincts, can pick up on things that are happening in nature and in the atmosphere that man cannot readily see/identify. Some animals use eco-location like the bats which we have been eradicating and now the mosquito population (and diseases they carry) has increased significantly! Some have electro-magnetism – like the butterfly. Some have pheromones – like the ants who are better economists than many of those in power today! Some have Magneto-reception – like the dogs and some birds who have a 'built-in GPS' and can detect magnetic fields. Meanwhile, for those who depend on man-made GPS, if there is the slightest glitch, then you will be led by it to the bushes, the sea or some remote destination they had no intention of reaching!

This is why man must always be spiritually connect to God, that we can discern the fourteen (14) opposite seasons, thus knowing how to plan and prepare for disaster.

There are too many people calling themselves specialists in whom political leaders are putting their trust, who are causing billions to go to waste and thus bringing nothing to the table. Meanwhile, many have a problem giving the poor a tax break; saying they can't afford it, when the tax break would barely be a drop in the bucket and would not even be missed!

For every natural problem there is a spiritual root. Until we get that understanding, we will always be changing leaders and looking for change and end up disappointed.

Change, and more so a mindset change, can only come through God! Sometimes it comes through painful experiences and I believe that the time is coming that many who are deemed the 'well-learned' will be humbled, because God is about to use some simple things and people to bring global change. Christians cannot afford to fall in that position. Many Christians have fallen into carnality and are living much like the un-regenerated person. They call themselves Christians but live more by and for human opinion. They are still drinking milk when they should be having solid food!

If Christians don't rise up and get to the next level, then there are some serious crises ahead! Every Christian needs to examine him/herself and see what impact he/she is really making! We should be the head but now we are positioned for the tail.

Victory Starts in the Mind

As the nation's athletes, coaches and management team prepare for the Olympics, each one of them must understand that this Olympics will be a mind game, and we cannot rely on past victories, neither can we become complacent or brag that we are a talented nation. We instead have to commit our work and talents to God and remember that He is the one, according to Deuteronomy 8: 18 that gives us the power to get wealth.

Remember that defeat, fear, doubt and even victory all begin in the mind. So, in order to become victorious we must first:

See the victory in your mind. Run the race in your mind and see yourself winning it.

Believe that you are the best, because God said so. When you step out on the track or field, know and believe that there is no one else on the field better than you at what you do.

Speak to your mind to line up (Psalm 121) and remember that your help comes from the Lord.

In a race, only one will get the gold. You have to run in a way that you obtain it. (1 Corinthians 9: 24)

You have to be disciplined in all ways, bringing your body into subjection. Master self-discipline, self-denial and self-control in order to get the gold. (1 Corinthians 9: 27)

Lay aside anything that hinders our progress – sin, parties, pride, friends – anything necessary to ensure that you are focused on the goal. (Hebrews 12: 1)

The Other Side of the Race

Before a race can be won in the natural/physical realm, it must first be won in the invisible/Spiritual realm. (Exodus 17: 8) This means that your prayers, your vows, your Tithe, your Fasting, your petitions and counter-petitions to the Lord, as well as the positive words that you speak can make a huge impact on your efforts to attain victory.

Every fear and doubt, obstacle and hindrance must first be overcome in the mind. Words are powerful! Everything was created by way of a spoken word! By principle, everything, good or bad, begins with a spoken word! So our team has to cover itself from the negative words of the media and competitors, and ask God to help them to overcome their personal fear. Remember, the enemy will say you are not good enough, fast enough or strong enough, but you must realize that your mountain is more afraid of you than you are of it!

Remember that your body reacts to your mind. Fear may say "I cannot make it" "I am going to make a false start" "I feel fatigue!" "I am not fit enough!" "I am a little third-world unknown, I am not as good as the first world athletes!" BUT, don't believe those lies! You must take charge of your mind, not have your mind control you. Your mind must obey your instructions! Just speak to your mind and say, "Mind, line up. We are the best!"

Start to create a picture in your mind. See the gold! See the victory! Write your victory speech! Get a picture of yourself as a winner and put it up in your house and declare yourself a winner daily!

Pray this prayer daily.

Heavenly Father, through Jesus Christ, thank you for the gifts, talents and abilities you have given me. I decree and declare that this is my year and this is my season. I will not be defeated, the gold is mine and the glory and power are Yours! You promised me that I can do all things through Christ who strengthens me and I stand on it now. I command my body to line up for victory now. I refuse to be distracted by negative words! Instead, I press toward the mark, for my higher calling in you, through you. Guide me and give me new tactics and strategies. Remove all plots, plans and obstacles from my path and I command victory now for myself and the team, oneness, unity and peace. Amen.

Your Mind Is Your Weapon Against Poverty

The mind is one of the most important parts of any human being. What we think and speak on a daily basis are critical and impacts our existence significantly. Success and failure both begin in the mind. If we paint a picture of poverty, joblessness and hopelessness and study that picture daily, or if in your mind you believe that your only option is to beg, or be a prostitute or to yield to a life of crime than that's the manifestation you will experience – it is exactly what will happen.

God created each of us with the ability to think of great ideas, solutions and inventions. All great inventions come from a thought which manifests when we move by faith. Take for example, famous African-American scientist and inventor George Washington Carver. He was born into slavery in Diamond, Missouri, around 1864. The exact year and date of his birth are unknown. Carver went on to become one of the most prominent scientists and inventors of his time, as well as a teacher at the Tuskegee Institute. Carver devised over 100 products using one major crop—the peanut—including dyes, plastics and gasoline. One of his many quotes states: "I love to think of nature as an unlimited broadcasting station, through which God speaks to us every hour, if we will only tune in."

Our parents and grandparents made their own coconut oil for cooking and would use it also as a lotion of sorts or as hair grease. We made our own sugar from cane. Practically every household had someone who could make guava jelly or orange marmalade. To beat the heat, we made and sold "sky juice" from the man with the push cart. The "sky juice" evolved into bag juice and the push cart entered the racing circuit through the creation of the Push Cart Derby. We are innovative and poverty is no excuse for not producing. There is a saying that "necessity is the mother of invention" – that statement clearly lets us know that within poverty is the potential for you to be an inventor!

The very dirt/soil you are standing on has the potential to be world class building material.

If other nations can come into our nation broke and then ultimately become millionaires, then there is something wrong with the way we think. Negativity is contagious and sometimes we have to leave not just our families, but the very community in order to see the positive picture. If, for example, a person sees gambling as his/her only way out, then even when they get an idea/solution, they will either gamble it away or think that the only way to fund it is to gamble. Furthermore, if we walk with thieves, we will begin to steal, if we walk with wise, we will become wiser, if we walk with fools, we will become foolish. Your environment influences your mind and the state of your mind determines your action/inaction.

People are always looking at the politicians as their savior and deliverer which is wrong. God is our Savior and Deliverer. In our minds, we must see and understand that they are servants of the people and not our masters, and so the people are always disappointed. Handouts give way for manipulation. We have the authority to create our own employment and change our community.

Check and see that for the last century the only ideas our politicians have had is to pass laws and shackle the peoples and bring greater oppression on the people. Because of the state of our leaders' minds, there is no vision and as such, the people are perishing.

Solutions

- ✓ Reduce the purchase of "brand name" items – including phones, clothing, shoes, and flat screen televisions - and live simply. What you save you can use to start a business. Use your life experience and turn it into a book or a movie. These days you can make a short movie using your phone.

- ✓ Write down on paper the ideas God has given/gives to you and start small.

- ✓ When you want the blessings of God, present something to Him so He can bless it. If you sit down doing nothing, God can't bless you. (Deuteronomy 28: 12; Deuteronomy 15: 10)

- ✓ Always think and speak positively every day. Stop speaking negatively – "the economy is bad"; "there are no jobs"; "nobody wants me"; "I am broke". Speak positive things/speak life – "I am the next successful CEO", "I am a successful entrepreneur"; "this is the best day/week/year/ of my life to date"; wealth and increase belongs to me and it comes to me today."

The Power of Positive Thinking

The mind is one of the most powerful tools a human being possesses. It is the area wherein we encounter our daily battles; and when we overcome those battles there is great success!

II Corinthians 10 outlines the warfare we encounter on a daily basis such as fear, lack of self-confidence, rejection, difficulty learning and/or understanding and numerous strongholds that attack our imagination. Philosophy is one such example of a weapon that often attacks the mind. A philosophical mindset focuses on logic, ethics, the metaphysical matters and trying to understand the deeper issues of life without seeking for the answers from the true source who is God!

If, for example, we view crime and violence from that standpoint, we will never solve the problem. If a psychiatrist or psychologist deemed someone mentally unstable and prescribed a particular medication and things either remained the same or became worse, would they continue to prescribe the same medication? If they increased the dosage and still nothing changed, then what would they do? Would they further increase the dosage or make a referral? Would they continue treat this individual without result only to keep their hands attached to his/her wallet – as was seen in Mark 5: 25 regarding the woman with the issue of blood. It was not until she became bankrupt seeking medical advice that she realized that her mind also needed to be renewed so that she could receive the healing she needed. She did not see that there was an alternative until her back was against the wall!

Here is an interesting question. Don't you think that after 12 years the doctors would have realized that there was really nothing they could do to deal with this particular situation? Would they not have realized that their knowledge and logic was not enough to address the matter? Could it be that they only wanted a steady source of income?

Inaccurate diagnoses of national or individual problems carry serious economic and legal ramifications and other serious side effects!

The difference between success and failure is the mindset, not academic qualifications nor levels of human intelligence. Even if party leaders change, without a renewing of the mind the old haunts and strongholds will continue to hinder the nation. So much so that even when there is a political change, after a while, the nation will begin to cry out for the former Administration to return, and so the cycle continues.

Further to this, if the Church Leaders are not making an impact on the nation it is not as a result of a need for more academically qualified theologians, it is in fact the need for mental renewal (according to Romans 12: 2) on both sides – the Church Leaders and the nation both need a Revelation from God!

Belief vs. Principles

Regardless of our varying beliefs, principles are key and go beyond a person's belief! When people are desperate for change, they don't care in whom you believe, once the principle is workable they will accept it.

Interestingly, once we each have a personal belief then we are automatically a part of politics, because every belief system has its view on how people should be governed. One definition of "politics" is "a person's beliefs about how a country should be governed." Another is "the winning and using of power to govern society."

Wherever and whomever we are, we cannot exclude politics from our daily lives. What we need however, are politicians who will live, walk and function according to Isaiah 11: 2 – 5.

What We Need

We need positive minds that are hopeful; without doubt, confident that will encourage someone else on a daily basis that 'We can make it! It doesn't matter what we are facing, we can make it!'

Philippians 4: 8 says, "Finally, brethren, whatever things are true, whatever things *are* noble, whatever things *are* just, whatever things *are* pure, whatever things *are* lovely, whatever things *are* of good report, if *there is* any virtue and if *there is* anything praiseworthy — meditate on these things" for *success*!

Chapter 13

VISION NOT SIGHT

Many people want to be part of a finished work, but often shy away from the building process! Very few want to be a part of something that is being established. They prefer to be a part of something that is already established and is – in their eyes – flourishing.

Let us recognize that to be a part of a vision or work that is 'under construction' gives us the opportunity to i) bring out and exercise our gifts and talents to the fullest; ii) allows us the privilege of being able to see and benefit from the groundwork, appreciate the work and vision, and experience the benefits, joys and satisfaction of the finished product when construction is complete.

Interestingly, during the building of a vision, we often ask the help of others with the expertise to help with the building process and to volunteer their time, gifts and talents; but because they don't see the vision, and even think that it is heading nowhere, they walk away and toward what they feel is a better 'investment' when God was trying to build them a future too! They could have been the next CEO or Chairperson within the vision, and their participation could also have secured a future for their children. There are those who are highly qualified, but feel that the small thing they see would be a waste of their time and ability so they walk away or show very little interest. If those who are not working in these times would find a small struggling organization and offer their

time and expertise to the building of that organization, they may be surprised to see the future they were building, and they may even contribute to their own employment or entrepreneurship in the future! Forsake not small beginnings! Every large organization started small.

In small organizations, many may see disorder, but disorder is an opportunity for a person to exercise their skill and expertise and bring the order needed! Maybe what is missing from the organization is you!

From time to time people talk about Warren Buffett, Donald Trump, Bill Gates and many other local 'movers and shakers'; and they would want to be affiliated with these persons. Truth be told, they have endured great struggles, rejection and many failed attempts. A great deal of their wealth comes out of investing in what others deem insignificant.

Every great businessman looks for those who have been tested and proven to be loyal and will stand in times of hardship rather than those who will connect only to share in the glory!

The Dark and Muddy Places

Oftentimes people look for their blessings in a place they feel is successful; and they look to people they believe are within or above their class. But the Bible lets us know that often our blessings are found in the dark and muddy places.

The dark places refer to those areas that we feel are insignificant and the muddy places are those places or persons we scorn or look down on or in which we see very little value. The inner city, the children's homes, retirees and the homeless are a few examples. Also included in this group are the broke, bankrupt, jobless, prostitutes, prisoners. By the way, God does not increase or multiply anything unless it is broken. (Matthew 6: 41 – 44) Joseph was a prisoner, Esther was an orphan, Ruth was a widow, Daniel was a slave and all these individuals became great deliverers.

The reason most nations are struggling is that they have a one-track mind; they are looking for change while doing the same thing over and over. Even our politicians employ the same methods and types of people every time. Even within the Church, persons choose where they go to church based on whom they want to 'rub shoulders' with, the beauty of the stained glass windows or how big and established they feel a particular church may be. Very few go where the Lord is sending them – where God wants to use them to build and prosper – so they die spiritually and miss out on the opportunity to fully become all they can be. Recognize that it is not about what we choose, but what God has chosen for us which is always better than anything we could choose.

In Genesis 22, there were many mountains in the area that Abraham could have chosen to climb, but God told him a specific mountain to go up and offer sacrifice (worship). It was on that specific mountain that the ram was caught in the bush so that Abraham could use it as his sacrifice to God. God made the provision!

Do You Want The Greater Vision?

Many times people tend to brag about the vision they have and want to pursue. But in order to pursue vision, one's vision has to die for the greater vision! We can look at the life of Elisha. He was a middle manager on his father's farm. In order for him to pursue greater vision, he had to walk away from everything, and he had to ensure that there was nothing left for him to look back to as a distraction. Sometimes God has to move you from your very family members, friends, associates and even your community in order to prepare you for the greater vision. Every vision that God has given you has a mentor assigned to prepare you for the vision. Elijah/Elisha, Ruth/Naomi, Esther/Mordecai.

Mentorship is important because there will be some Jordans ahead that you must cross and in order to do so, either your mentor has to go before you or your mentor's spirit has to rest upon you. Crossing Jordan requires wisdom, knowledge and understanding. Jordan is a dangerous place and not many make it across. In order to cross Jordan, you cannot afford to be distracted or focus on your personal vision and problems. If you are focusing on your problem rather than ensuring you serve and learn from your mentor, you will miss valuable insight and lessons that will allow you the wisdom, knowledge and understanding you need to move forward.

There are a lot of times believers miss God's will because they become pre-occupied with their own problems. You cannot take up a mantle unless you are being mentored and prepared – whether in the secular or in ministry. A

mantle is always something that falls, and you cannot pick up a mantle if you are not at the place serving and submitting to your mentor!

Regardless of the vision, promises and prophecies that God gives you, if you don't have a mentor that unlocks and births what is inside of you it will never come to fruition. God never sends a person on a journey unless preparation has been made beforehand. The anointing is important because it will protect you on the journey. One can choose to create one's own blessing and call it God's blessing because they want to avoid the processing. However, in various Times and Seasons one will go through, if one is not fully prepared, one will crumble under pressure.

- ✓ Which mantle are you qualified to take up and carry?

- ✓ Which mentor are you serving?

- ✓ Are you focusing on your vision or the greater vision?

- ✓ Are you willing to give up your dreams and visions to get a bigger one?

- ✓ When Elisha took up Elijah's mantle, why did he tear his clothes in two?

- ✓ Do you think you have what it takes to cross Jordan?

Chapter 14

GRACE

Grace, Favor and Mercy

We often talk about Grace, Favor and Mercy, but do we really understand what these words mean? No one can live without Grace. The obstacles, challenges and problems we face on a daily basis, could not/cannot be resolved without Grace, Favor and Mercy.

The word **"Grace"** simply put, means "getting something we do not deserve; unmerited favor; mercy and compassion."

God's greatest act Grace that has been given/extended to us is the ability to receive salvation which is available through faith. (Ephesians 2: 8 – 9)

Grace is what opens doors to us when we are not qualified and t gives us promotion we don't even deserve. That is why we must be humble on a daily basis and show someone mercy and compassion; without Grace, we would not be in the position we are now.

Have you ever been in a selection process for a position or a competition of any kind? In your mind, you didn't think you would reach very far or had the talent to go through it, or would even get to a certain level; but it is Grace allowed you to come out on top and it even surprised you!

Oftentimes there are persons who are involved in accidents of one kind or another, and they are the only ones to survive. Some people will tell them they are lucky, but it is not luck – it is the Grace of Jesus Christ that kept them and has given them another chance. The main reason that you are alive now and are able read this very article is the Grace of God!

Favor occurs when the requirements and protocols are waived for you. For example, Esther, Daniel and Joseph all walked in great favor and the kings loved or became endeared to them. When we were going to school, some students, or maybe you, were called the 'Teacher's Pet'. God gave favor with the teacher. Maybe when everybody else was failing you just zoomed right through every class and exam with flying colors.

Mercy occurs when one deserves punishment and God withholds His hand and instead extends His love to them. For example, God sparing Jamaica from a category 5 hurricane; or in the legal circles, God would allow a magistrate to rule in your favor rather than against you; or in any organization with which you transact business, even when you are in default they still extend mercy to you to settle the matter by way of a Grace period.

Gifts and Talents

Quite often, many will see the gifts and talents of others and shower them with praises and accolades! Look at people like Michael Jordan, Patrick Ewing, Usain Bolt, Bob Marley, Serena Williams and President Barack Obama. It is God's Grace and His Favor

Know that no leader at any level can truly be successful without God's Grace, Favor and Mercy; and that is what will bring prosperity within a nation. Every leader has to ensure that God's Grace, Favor and Mercy never leaves them, for when they do, there is sure defeat!

Success, growth and great achievement can only come through Grace. (John 15: 5) This is why we MUST abide in God. Regardless of how successful a person is, without God's grace, the qualifications and academic achievements mean nothing.

Many times the success of an organization hinges on the presence of a few righteous people in the organization who have Grace and Favor on their lives! We see it with Jacob where Laban prospered simply by having Jacob working for him. Oftentimes, when these few righteous leave, the organization crashes or goes through a slow, painful death. So extending Grace to a servant of God can save your life. They are your insurance; and that is why you must be careful in how you treat a servant of God.

Paul reminds us, in 1 Corinthians 15: 9 – 10, that although he is the least of the Apostles, it is the Grace of God that has allowed him to accomplish all the work the Lord allowed him to do for Him.

There are many times people will take on Titles and put themselves in certain positions; but it is the Grace of God that sanctions it all. So if God's grace for the title or position is not with you then don't take it on; you would be heading for trouble!

God wants to extend Grace, Favor and Mercy particularly to those who are sick – to heal their bodies. You need to begin praying for Grace, Favor and Mercy on a daily basis - for your family, community, nation and the nation's leaders.

The Power of Grace

During this Easter Season, while we recognize that not everyone celebrates the significance of the season for various reasons, the key thing is to simply be grateful, appreciative and thankful that Jesus did come and lay His life down for us all!

The main fact that we are alive today is as a result of the fact that He came and extended to us His Grace!

Regardless of the spiritual condition one is in, it is God's grace that allows us hope, and grants us the free favor of God. Even as people ridicule God, and even challenge Him to do something drastic to them as proof of His existence, it is the grace of God extended to them that keeps them.

The grace of God allows us to have the Favor and Goodness of God. For example, have you ever been promoted to a position for which you are not qualified or for which you were not the favorite applicant, but you got the job and are doing well? That was the favor of God!

Many may think that success and prosperity has to do with one's academic qualifications! Think about a company making super-profits and exceed financial forecasts. Then you hear the executives of the organization being interviewed and they would credit their success to their own academic achievements, their PR Team or some other thing without acknowledging God. *Not so*! It is God's grace that allowed them to get profits, wisdom, knowledge, and strategies for their business!

When God's grace and favor are removed from any individual or organization – regardless of a person's level of intelligence and academic qualifications, there is going to be failure. Nothing can stop that if God's grace and favor are removed!

Some will say that God's grace favor and goodness are not fair, but God extends grace to whomever He chooses, whenever He chooses.

There are those lawyers who have never lost a case; athletes who have never lost a race. It is God's grace and favor! It is that same grace and favor that allows a commoner to marry a king! (Esther in the Bible, Kate Duchess of Cambridge) Even for a black man to become president of a nation that was always ruled by white men – that is favor also!

Grace and Leadership

A lot of people – particularly leaders – are failing, because they failed to acknowledge God's grace. It is God's grace that allowed a David to remove a Goliath and stop him from threatening a nation. David used five stones – which symbolized grace – to defeat that giant. We need leaders who are not afraid to use Go's principles to remove giants – debt poverty, crime hopelessness!

Walking in God's grace allows us to walk in His presence, His rest, His goodness, His mercy, wisdom, truth and discernment to successfully lead a nation. Even more so, many nation leaders have become extremely stressed, wearied, tired and sometimes sick! More often than not, it is a lack of grace that brings these results!

It was the grace of God that brought a nation out of oppression and bondage; and not only brought them out debt free, but with wealth in hand! (Exodus 3, 11, 12)

Grace brings protection of those who are faithful to God from the plagues of life! (Exodus 3)

Grace allows those God has called and chosen to carry out His assignment. Even Noah – who God chose – to prepare an ark with the capacity to save many who are willing. The Ark can symbolize the preparation of something that is to bring protection, deliverance, and provision in hard times! An Ark cannot sail on dry land – it is going to take a flood. There are many people still in this earth that God is using to prepare for a time to come! Likewise, light has little effect during the daytime – the light shines in the dark!

Not everyone has the same capacity for the same things. Many times leaders are criticized and compared with others, but grace for the task of leadership is given based on their calling. (Romans 12: 3 & 6)

Many times people take on positions onto themselves because they feel that they can do it; but if a person does not have the grace for the position, they would do well not to touch it!

It is God's grace that keeps us fresh and flourishing!

It is the grace of God that keeps us from falling. (2 Corinthians 12: 7)

It is God's grace that causes us to have the opportunity for the abundant life!

Whether you are an Atheist, Buddhist, Muslim or Christian, it is God's grace that keeps us all alive on a daily basis! Never underestimate the power of Grace!

God's Grace Makes Us Great

No nation, organization or individual can be great without the grace of God. It is the grace of God that allows any entity or person to be great and to accumulate riches, wealth and power.

These days we are seeing many trample on the grace of God. Some are even using the very profits from their organization to try to weaken God's moral values within the earth. Many may believe that the success they enjoy is only a result of their efforts and intellect. However, as is alluded in Deuteronomy 17 and 18, it is in fact the grace of God that allows us to enjoy success at any level.

When we take God's grace for granted, we will begin to see the shifting of His favor from our lives collectively and individually. All eyes should be on the first world nations that are now falling from grace. When one falls from grace, it affects everything within the society. Even great 'football-centered' nations such as Brazil, France and Argentina are now experiencing the favor and grace slipping away from them. If the smaller countries that are deemed insignificant, continue to fear God and not take His grace for granted, the will undoubtedly experience success and God's promise for riches, honor and life. Those who take it for granted will without doubt, come to the realization that the cemeteries and morgues will be good investments!

I encourage every individual, organization and nation to do a self-examination from time to time. Each needs to revisit, where they are and where they come from, because we often forget that it is in fact the grace of God that allows us to reach different levels of success! Even if a person gains wealth by illegal means (because no business is innocent) then recognize that it is the grace of God why you didn't get caught at that time!

People need to ask the themselves, regardless of their profession, when they were struggling to pass their exams, struggling to find a job, struggling to be selected to get a promotion and even to become leaders of nations or organizations what they went through and how did they make it through.

Where God's grace takes us, neither man's degree, intellect, or contacts can take us there. As far as we can go, God's grace can take us further. It is critical for us to trust the Lord to direct our path. (Proverbs 3: 5 – 6) Many are ignore God's grace, Word and precepts and are making choices and decisions which will bring them in a path of destruction and defeat! Men rule, but God overrules! Men make decrees and change laws, but God makes new decrees and upholds His laws!

Recently, I was watching the celebration of the legalization of same-sex marriages. But what the pundits and the global media networks do not understand is that this has also awakened the sleeping giants and there is about to be political shaking ahead. It will also affect other nations. So while some Christians were crying for defeat, it will in fact be victory and the True Intercessors have been awakened. Meanwhile, God is going to use it to expose the fakes within the kingdom. So there are interesting days ahead.

Do Good Work

1 Timothy 6: 17 – 18 reminds us, "Command those who are rich in this present age not to be haughty, nor to trust

in uncertain riches but in the living God, who gives us richly all things to enjoy. Let them do good, that they be rich in good works, ready to give, willing to share,"

Each person to whom God gives His grace to be wealthy, should be good stewards by sharing with others – an investment that will give eternal dividends. Every rich man should know that values change. Earthly riches are only as good as the present value. What might be valuable to day may have no value tomorrow. That is why we must do good! Greed is stopping progress globally. God wants us to pursue these six principles – Righteousness, Godliness, Faith, Love, Patience and Gentleness – these bring true riches. Money should never master man. Man should master money!

When the wealthy begin to use their money to do good, the world would be a better place. The wealthy especially need to tread carefully, because we are entering into a new season and you never know what the next season will bring!

Chapter 15

WINNING IN THE MARKETPLACE

Every believer's ethical duty and diligence in the marketplace is to perform as though serving Christ even as counterparts/coworkers may not be Christian.

Many times, Christians are the most difficult people to work within an organization; which ultimately sends the wrong signals or message; and it turns people off from employing them. (Ephesians 6: 5 – 9)

With the global problems being faced by every sector, including the financial, security and political arenas, and if the children of light don't rise up now, there are going to be some dark days ahead globally. Matthew 5: 16 says, "Let your light so shine before men, that they may see your good works and glorify your Father in heaven."

The children of light should be allow their light to shine within their organization, bring solutions for the organization without compromising. The main fact that they are part of the organization means that God has placed them there for a purpose; and if that purpose is not being fulfilled, then that door of access is going to close. Such persons need to ask themselves the question, 'Why am I here?'

Many secular organizations make decisions, which bring great hardship, security risks and/or suffering, while those who know the truth - the children of light - keep silent because of fear. They should not fail to carry out their function in helping society. If fear gets the better of them, then we are going to see anarchy, more job losses, poverty or more human trafficking! More laws will be put in place to violate Biblical Principles and our beliefs - regardless of our faith.

The Christian Boss

The Christian boss should lead by example in whatever area they are placed to manage. They can't be like the secular leader. Their main source from which to draw strength and direction in order to carry out their daily activities and to deal with the daily challenges must be GOD!

Many times, it is said that Christian bosses are worse than the unsaved ones. Christian boss, you MUST show mercy and compassion. You must understand that you are accountable to God, in the same way that God would hold a Pastor responsible for the flock. (Ephesians 6: 9)

Galatians 6: 10 reminds us "Therefore, as we have opportunity, let us do good to all, especially to those who are of the **household** of faith."

We need to look out for each other as Christians, not to become a clique, but to unite so that others will see the right example of the light!

Christian bosses should not exploit the poor. You cannot be like the secular bosses who gain their wealth by dishonest means. The main reason why the world is going through this dark period is as a result of the fact that the children of light have compromised for fame, money and power. Now we are reaping the benefits of that. Many have gotten access to make a difference but they have compromised.

The marketplace is crying out for light! Remember, children of light must use their money so that God gets the glory; feeding the poor, giving scholarships to children of those who truly need it. According to James 5: 3, we ought not to lay up our treasures for ourselves while people suffer. You have been blessed to be a blessing.

Christian Politicians

Every Christian politician should study Matthew 5: 13 – 16. They should understand that they are Kingdom Citizens and the metaphor of salt and light indicate the citizen's influence for good, as they work in the secular society. Any believer who no longer holds on to the Word of God, is of no use to God or man! Each Christian politician must recognize that they are to be reflectors of light which come from God. No light, if it is the proper one, can be hid! No one who walks in light, should embrace darkness. All should learn from Daniel. With all the plots from political associates, he remained true to God without compromise. Daniel brought solutions and he never bowed to corruption.

When children of light see themselves as servants of Christ first, then the Spirit of Excellence will come upon us, to help your organization, your first goal is to please God. Then God will please the people.

Every employee must deal with his/her organization with honest, excellent service. Remember that your reward may not come from man in a Performance Appraisal or increase in salary; but in due season God will reward you.

Hope for Struggling Businesses

" . . . He said to Simon, "Launch out into the deep and let down your nets for a catch." But Simon answered and said to Him, "Master, we have toiled all night and caught nothing; nevertheless at Your word I will let down the net." And when they had done this, they caught a great number of fish, and their net was breaking. . ."

Despite your circumstances today – your business might be struggling, sales are low and slow, the bills are piling up and you are being pressured by lenders – there is always hope for a large catch. In order to receive a miracle that will turn your circumstances around, you need to seek for an instruction, because there is always something that you have in possession that can turn things around.

Before one can experience a turnaround within your business or the nation:

- ✓ First, your mindset must begin to change.

 ✓ Second, obedience to instruction is key.

 ✓ Third, you must be willing to be taught by people who are not a part of your profession or even those deemed 'unqualified'. Would an economist take advice from a 'hustler'? Would a doctor take advice from a wholesale owner on how to run successful practice/business? Would a fisherman take instructions from a carpenter on how to be an effective entrepreneur?

In order to turn around your struggling business, you must be willing to do something beyond 'the norm'; think deeper, think bigger, increase your faith and be willing to take risks! Even in areas you have failed before, be willing to try again!

Put Local First

There is a dangerous trend that is now coming to the fore in many nations as a result of the financial situations. Nations are now giving citizenship to those who have the monetary substance, and this is a dangerous precedence which has the potential for global security problems.

What nations should be doing is creating an environment for local business to thrive! Local businesses provide the opportunities to service the communities. They are the ones who ought to be getting tax breaks, and the alleviation of certain restrictions.

If we desire to see growth in any industry we must ensure that we create the environment for nationals to support and also to reap and enjoy those benefits. How many are afforded the basic provisions, pleasures and choices of the land in which they live – and especially with their families?

We must engage the principle where we take care of family first! Visitors will always come and go but family will always remain family! We have to believe in ourselves that what we have is of value, and change always begins within and not from the outside.

Our nation should not be passing laws because of external influencers; laws must be passed when there is the need for the betterment of the people. Leaders must be willing to engage in self-sacrifice. Leaders cannot expect the people do what they are not willing to do. They must listen to the people, because numerous solutions lie within the people.

Cast Your Net and Don't Give Up

When you cast your net and nothing comes up, don't give up, there are lessons to be learnt. You are getting wiser. Your faith is getting stronger. God may be trying to get your attention so that you put your trust in Him. God is trying to change your mindset with the tactics and strategies of fishing. It is not luck or your qualifications that were giving you success in the past. It was in fact God's favor that caused you to succeed all along. God may have a bigger plan for your business. He wants to expand it with new products and ideas. Some people are going through problems because He wants to change their profession and re-route them – getting them into a different geographical area.

Despite how dismal things may seem, there is always something you possess in your physical or spiritual house that can change the game for you. Your situation is not generally as bad as it may seem. In no time, you could go from zero to hero.

Oftentimes, nations tend to focus on improving infrastructure and ignore the invaluable human resources.

When God is going to bless a nation, the vessel He pours into first is the human vessel, who have the ability and capacity to engage change!

I write this to encourage all business owners that are planning to call it a day. Don't give up – launch out into the deep.

12 Daily Habits for Successful Entrepreneurs

On a daily basis:

1. Engage in Prayer and reading the Word of God. (Matthew 6: 33)

2. Exercise

3. Eat Breakfast – eat healthy foods and drink lemon juice or vinegar in a glass of water each day.

4. Use the instructions you have received in Prayer and the Word to arrange or rearrange your day.

5. Have midday prayer (12 noon – 1 pm) and use that time period to motivate your staff and set new goals and objectives.

6. Schedule time for income-generating activities – includes your donations and tithes.

7. Follow up with faithful clients and customers and this will bring re-orders, new orders and resolve outstanding customer service issues.

8. Check up on or spend time with the family.

9. Check up on or touch base with your Spiritual mentors.

10. Declare Psalm 112, Psalm 91, Psalm 121, and Matthew 6: 9 – 13 upon your life and your family. Ask the Lord to put a hedge of protection around your family and business.

11. Pray for your customers' welfare. Get a list of your customers and place your hand on it daily and pray for them.

12. Always reward faithful staff members and let them know you care.

Further to all this:

- ✓ Dedicate one day per week to Fasting for your business and learn about the different seasons within the Bible.

- ✓ Operate with mercy and compassion in business dealings and debt write-offs.

Limit Stress in Your Organization

As times become increasingly difficult, stress is also on the increase. The greatest desires of man today are to be debt-free and at peace. The environment today is tense with stress as many are increasingly concerned about tomorrow! As a result of the increasing stress levels, many people try many different things in order to lay hold of peace.

According to David S. Walonick, Ph.D.in his 1993 paper on Causes and Cures of Stress in Organizations, "... Arnold and Feldman (1986) define stress as "the reactions of individuals to new or threatening factors in their work environment" (p. 459). Since our work environments often contain new situations, this definition suggests that stress in inevitable. This definition also highlights the fact that reactions to stressful situations are individualized, and can result in emotional, perceptual, behavioral, and physiological changes."

Politicians and Legislators even add to the stress with and then put laws in place in order to curtail our response to their oppression.

Jesus outlined in Matthew 26: 25 – 34 that worry (stress) is a distraction and that it was unreasonable, unnatural, unhelpful, unnecessary and unbelieving.

Thus, we are not to become distracted from the substantial issues of life over less important matters such as what we will eat or wear. We are the only creation of God's that worries. God provides for the birds and we more valuable than they are. God provides for the needs of His own.

While stress is found in all levels of society, let us look at some occupations that carry extreme levels of stress.

- ✓ Police
- ✓ Doctors
- ✓ Nurses
- ✓ Teachers
- ✓ National Leaders
- ✓ Church Leadership/Clergy
- ✓ Tax Collectors
- ✓ Correctional Officers

In order to have a less stressful environment, it is critical for leaders in every organization to play an active role in the process of reducing stress. So they could start by looking at more than just the academic qualifications of an individual to place him or her as one of its customer service representatives, for example, and look also at the person's ability/gift to engage their customers pleasantly, professionally and respectfully.

They must also create the environment that is conducive to a pleasant, experience with the organization; that is, set the right atmosphere so that customers/clients fell comfortable and confident doing business with them even if they may be under financial pressures.

Rules, Laws and Regulations

All these must be carefully thought out and evaluated before they are even brought to the fore. A customer in default of payments ought not to be treated with less respect than the person who is not, because tough times can hit anyone and you never know when the tables may turn.

Debt Collectors and Loan Officers should not always seek to intimidate those in default. It adds nothing but stress and makes their jobs that much harder. Instead, one of their main strategies could be to encourage and motivate their customers, and where possible, visit them to see how they can help to direct them on that issue. They might be pleasantly surprised to see the solutions that would come out of that!

A manager, sitting in a comfortable chair in the office with the Air Condition making rash or rushed decisions about those outside of his/her reality does not realize that it is not as comfortable for those about whom they make their decisions.

Service

Good customer service and a pleasant and professional environment will bring repeat business to your organization even where your product is not the best in quality by comparison; even when the prices are by comparison higher, because the service given makes a huge difference.

Technology has robbed many organizations of the personal touch that is so important to its customers. Today, when you call many organizations, we are met with the impersonal 'Press 1, Press 2' message; and after all that you hear, 'Message Full' or 'Goodbye'

Managers need to pretend to be an external customer and try to call their own offices and see what their Secretaries, Administrative Assistants or Personal Assistants are like to deal with!

Some of the big businessmen should attempt to call their companies to try get something rectified, and see what the experience is like and make adjustments where necessary.

There needs to be some serious adjustment and addition to the curriculum at the training level for the Police Force. They must be taught how to remain composed under pressure; how to treat the general public despite treatment by members of the public; how to respond to people and situations and help to bring positive change.

Christians! Use The Gifts In The Marketplace!

There are many resources that God has given Christians to build nations, organizations and even the marketplace. However, many are spending millions in the wrong places in order to get solutions for survival. The gifts are spiritual resources given to Christians for the *profit* of all. [**Profit** from the Greek term – "*sumphero*" which means "**to bring together, to benefit, to be advantageous"** (1 Corinthians 12: 7)

Spiritual gifts are not to be buried or hidden in the ground. (Matthew 25; Luke 19)   Many church leaders over the years have done a poor job of teaching their members who work in the marketplace – the public and private sectors – how to apply the spiritual gifts they possess, to daily situations they face, and how to use those gifts to build!

Surprisingly,   even   Christians   who   observe   other Christians using their God-given gifts call them evil or crazy! Yet they listen the horoscope, engage in tea leaf reading, tarot card readings, palm reading and use other medium and devices to gain information within the marketplace; and all these bring defilement!

The recent passing of the Flexi-Week law is an indication that Christians, wherever they are placed – need to utilize their God-given gifts to advise their employers and to make meaningful contributions. If even God rested from work, then we need also to follow suit. This will not help the economy, instead it will destroy the economy; and when the dust settles, we will see whether it is mammon or God's Word that will triumph!

It is critical now, more than ever, for those who possess the spiritual gifts to begin utilizing them; advise their organizations on business decisions.

Investment Strategies

It is very critical for whose within the private or public sectors to help those within their sectors to understand Times and Seasons – how, when, where and in what to invest! They proper direction when there is going to be Market Expansion and even to make other major decisions.

As the globe darkens, gifts and talents will be more valuable than even academic qualifications. God used men like Joseph, Daniel, Isaiah and Nehemiah to rebuild and reform nations!

Spiritual gifts go beyond religious beliefs. For example, many within the marketplace, God uses dreams and visions to speak to them for decision-making. But many are unable to interpret it or believe it is foolish and ignore the gifts; only to pay the price later! For example, God uses dreams to speak to us in six (6) ways.

  ✓ *To provide God's answers to questions*

  ✓ *To instruct us in the things of God*

  ✓ *To warn us about unseen danger*

  ✓ *To guide us away from wrongdoing*

- ✓ *To save our lives*

- ✓ *To keep us away from pride*

God is always speaking but are we listening? He speaks even to political leaders and kings – on how to run their Administration.

The following are some of the gifts given to help within the marketplace!

Leadership and Administration	Romans 12: 3 – 8 Used for modeling, superintending and developing human capital and systems
Teaching	Romans 12: 3 – 8 How to explain and apply truth. There is a difference between the gift of Teaching and Teaching as a profession. Not all Teachers have the gift to teach. Hence the problems in many of our schools today!
Giving	Romans 12: 3 – 8 The capacity to give beyond the normal expectation, supported by a willingness to do so and a high level of humility and grace without the expectation of something in return.

**Word of
Knowledge**   I Corinthians 12   Supernatural
Revelation of the Divine will and
Plan, insight or understanding of
Circumstances or a body of facts by

revelation that is without assistance
of any human resource. It involves
Moral wisdom for right living and
relationship. Word of Knowledge is
best used in counseling, interrogation
by Law Enforcement personnel, the
Medical Industry and it solves
problems.

Word of Wisdom   I Corinthians 12   Supernatural
perspective to ascertain Divine means
for accomplishing God's will in a
given situation.   Divinely given
power to appropriate spiritual
intuition in problem-solving. Gives
direction. Best used in negotiation,
the diplomatic, political and judicial
fields forecasting accurate economic
paths.

**Discernment of
Spirits**   1 Corinthians 12   Supernatural
power to detect the realm of the Spirit
and their activities. It reveals the
plans and purposes of the enemy and

his forces – plots, plans and intent. Best used within negotiations, security, fighting terrorism, new Businesses – revealing the persons actions and intents and whether or not they should be trusted. It prevents one from being deceived in

a relationship or by politicians' empty promises!

The Bible: Your Investment Guide

"However, we speak wisdom among those who are mature, yet not the wisdom of this age, nor of the rulers of this age, who are coming to nothing. But we speak the wisdom of God in a mystery, the hidden wisdom which God ordained before the ages for our glory" (2 Corinthians 2: 6 – 7)

Only the Spiritually mature can understand the wisdom of God. The wisdom of the world is foolishness compared to the wisdom of God. It is for this reason that the plans and advice of philosophers and advisors, who do not seek God, have come to naught. Many will employ the advice of the various money magazines for investment purposes – stocks, bonds and other investment portfolios. But the Bible is the most accurate tool for investment. It tells the Times and Seasons to invest, in what to invest, where to invest (including other countries) wisdom, integrity and solutions in business. It also gives keys to investment and it is your original blueprint in terms of investment. When one uses the word of God as a guideline to carry out transactions and abides by these principles, then one will experience growth, prosperity, increase in new investments, job creation, divine protection, abundance as well as reduction in crime, debt and security costs, particularly with guns and ammunition.

The days of wanting to create a prosperous economic environment by ignoring the principle of God – those days are over. Unless investors desire to renew their minds and have a new form of thinking many businesses, particularly the financial institutions are going to be seriously affected to the point of closing down. Very shortly, the number of faithful depositors that come into the branches each day will significantly decrease, and while the bank makes its profits from loans, that to will be in jeopardy.

If the social issues within the nation are not addressed for improvement – especially the dysfunction of the family in general; and if matters such as general grooming, etiquette, protocol, communication skills, self-esteem development and basic respect for the elders of the society are not promoted and addressed, then not only will the nation lose its basic moral fabric, but gambling, pornography and the sex trade will increase and those elements will not grow the economy. In fact, those will only propel crime, violence and poverty.

Tactics for Investment

Acquiring wealth comes as a result of putting vision into action with Divine direction and Biblical guidance. For example, for change to take place in the global economy, there needs to be an expansion of the job market. In order to get this expansion, it means that plans and ideas must be developed within. God requires every man to labor. It is time for every man to check and see their areas of struggle and identify the broken things within their community that need to be fixed. What conversations occur repeatedly on a daily basis? Those issues are either a source of pain or joy. Look around the various places that are being neglected and recognize that those places contain the wealth. Which areas of the general market do people avoid? This is where the wealth exists.

Never invest only in one organization. We have always heard the statement, 'never put your eggs in one basket." Ensure that your financial advisors are able to discern the times and seasons as well as the market conditions. Would you invest in something that has not yet been proven? Always invest in an organization where its managers are performers who are willing to change and learn, and are vigilant. Would you trust putting your money in the hands of profilers?

Invest in land. Purchase land and hold on to it, now is not the time to sell!
Invest in God-fearing countries and companies and communities that look dilapidated and broken down – it's where the wealth exists.

Finally, there is a shift about to take place within the marketplace. Israel is about to rise and it will become an investment paradise. There are a number of hidden treasures that are about to be revealed.

If the Western nations are wise, then they will recognize that now is the time to foster a relationship with Israel. Such nations will receive mutual benefits. We also need to watch Haiti, Egypt and the African nations. There will be great investment opportunities arising in those areas.

Chapter 16

SOWING TO WIN

"But God has chosen the foolish things of the world to put to shame the wise, and God has chosen the weak things of the world to put to shame the things which are mighty; and the base things of the world and the things which are despised God has chosen, and the things which are not, to bring to nothing the things that are" (1 Corinthians 1: 27 – 28)

Tithing

The carnal mind sees no value in Tithing. But the Spiritual mind recognizes and identifies its relevance and importance. The carnal mind would prefer to build up the economy on the foundation of gambling or immorality. Tithing affords us the capacity to receive the ideas and solution an original blueprints to build an economy.

When one tries to build a blueprint for a nation's economy on the basis of other nation's blueprints, then it shows a lack of creativity and originality and laziness. God created the economy before He created man – when He spoke all the elements into being and then placed man in it. Once man follows the precepts, laws and principles laid out by the Creator, then everything will fall into place.

Tithing speaks of one tenth and the number ten also speaks of completion, labor. We have ten fingers and we labor with them all. The number ten also represents the perfection of God's Divine order. Interestingly, these ten words - Law, Testimony, Ways, Precepts, Statutes, Commandments, Judgement, Path, Order, and Understanding are critical keys to a sound economy. They are the words the Lord used to direct man to effectively govern the earth. We must recognize and employ them daily.

Tithing opens your eyes to see the resources as well as how and where to invest them. It is not about being Christian or non-Christian. God commands everyone to Tithe. It honors God! Very shortly, regardless of the state of the economy, we are going to see the varying results in those organizations and individuals that tithe versus those that don't.

The Scriptures speak about the ten virgins - five wise and the five foolish. There is also the reference to the ten plagues and the importance of the ten days of consecration. In the Chinese numeral system, the symbol for the number ten is a Cross. In science, the number ten represents the element Neon. It is a gas within the atmosphere which is used in Neon signs, television tubes and can freeze things 3 times more than liquid hydrogen. Our numbering system is based on the number 10. In cricket, ten persons have to be bowled out before the other team can go in. The Bible speaks of the ten nations that will come together to rule the world. Even more interestingly, there were ten generations between Adam and Noah; and ten generations between Noah and Abraham.

According to Leviticus 27: 30 – 32, the tithe is holy and it belongs to God for establishing His kingdom. That it belongs to God means that it is to be used to establish His kingdom, feeding the poor, taking care of the priests as His earthly representatives. The reason the nation is suffering at this point is that the purpose for which the tithe is to be used is not taking place, so the priests and the poor now have to find alternative methods to sustain themselves. So the attention that they would give to the spiritual and other needs of the people under their care are being neglected as they make efforts to survive financially.

In II Chronicles 31, King Hezekiah led by example by calling a tithe amnesty – to restore the order of things, thereby allowing the priests to re-focus and fulfill their duties according to the instruction of God. This brought major economic revival in the nation!

How many politicians are truly Tithing?

Tithing is not for the Pastor to be rich, but for you to receive the blessings and wealth. Many who criticize tithing simply don't understand what this principle is about, nor do they seek to genuine understand. Yet, I am certain that they have no problems paying the dues and fees required to maintain membership in their clubs and other civic organizations. Tithing carries seven benefits that you will receive once you are faithful in this area. Tithing is an expression of honor to God. Where your money goes to determines where your honor lies. Tithing began in the Old Testament times and continues into the New Testament in Hebrews 7, and as such ought to continue today.

Many would prefer to see or have the church powerless. They know the value of money and that to be effective within a society, one must have money – financial resources. When the Church lacks the finance to carry out its functions, then other organization s pushing immorality begin to strive. There are billions going to enhance immorality while people refuse to tithe unto God. They prefer to tithe to immorality.

The 7 Benefits of Paying Tithes

There are a number of other principles that businessmen need to know and employ. Tithing is one such principle. 'Tithe' means 'one-tenth of one's income or produce'.

God has promised that in paying our Tithes, by doing that one thing for Him, He will do seven for us in return – He asks us to prove Him. He said:

1. "I will open the windows of heaven ..."

   What this means is that the Lord will give us New Businesses, New Investments,
   New Ideas and Initiatives to present, New Products on the Market and the Best Quality Staff to enable and enhance your vision.

2. "I will pour out for you a blessing ...!"

   This means God's power to produce in every area of your life. It also means Health, Wisdom, Knowledge and Interest on your Investment.

(NB The word 'Blessing' comes from the Hebrew word 'Barak')

3. "There shall be no room enough to receive ..."

This simply means expansion in every area!

4. "I will rebuke the Devourer for your sakes ..."

Who is the Devourer? The Devourer is the devil and what this statement means is that God will prevent loss by theft, fraud, sabotage, industrial action, and setbacks in Strategic Planning. He will ensure that everything is insured by Him. You will not make a loss; you will achieve your monthly budget and earn profits. You will have a good family life! He will protect you from accidents. You will have job security and good health. You will also benefit from high staff morale levels. Only God can protect you from the Devourer! (John 10: 10)

5. "Nor shall the vine fail to bear fruit for you in the field ..."

It does not matter what business you are in, He will prevent the devil from messing up your business – whether he attacks through witchcraft and other setbacks, which are designed to (and can) destroy your business.

✓ He will deal with your vine, the very source.

  ✓ He will ensure that your crop will not be dumped before the opportune time to harvest.

6. "…All nations will call you blessed …"

  You want to be well thought of in your land and your job. You want the promotion. God will promote you and establish your reputation.

Once you are not paying your Tithes – whether you are a Christian or not, there is no guarantee that the benefits and blessings of the Lord will be yours.

Obedience Is Key!

We must recognize that all visions are given by God, and it is He who gives us the power to get wealth (Deuteronomy 8: 17 – 18). By excluding Biblical Principles, it will not be long before you are totally destroyed by the Devourer!

How to Get That Hundred-Fold Return

No financial institution can or will give you a hundred-fold return. Only God's institution promises and can deliver it! Don't worry about the losses, no profit can be made without losses being incurred; but God always promises and gives us twice what was lost. (Job 42) So if you have ever lost anything, get ready for a hundred-fold return.

1. Seek God first in all things. Matthew 6: 33 tells us this. To seek means to inquire, require of, and research. You must be specific seek to fear Him first that is the beginning of wisdom. To seek does not only mean Prayers. It also means research some things, because God created everything. Revelation 4: 11, Colossians 1: 16, Ephesians 3: 9 also encourage us to put God first in everything. Your main focus must be kingdom-business; not your work, not your wife nor husband, not your children, but God must come first!

2. Prepare to meet the standard or qualification as set out in Mark 10: 29 – 30. "And Jesus answered and said, 'Verily I say unto you, there is no man that hath left house, or brethren, or sisters, or father, or mother, or wife, or children, or lands, for my sake, and the gospel's. But he shall receive an hundredfold now in this time, houses, and brethren, and sisters, and mothers, and children, and lands, with persecutions; and in the world to come eternal life.'". Once you have met the standards, you are in line for a hundred-fold return. Jesus will be a debtor to no one! The blessing He gives will far outweigh material loss and persecution incurred in service for Him!

3. Have faith! You must believe without the shadow of a doubt that God will fulfill His promises and do what He says He will do. Mark 11: 23 – 24 says, "For verily I say unto you, that whosoever shall say unto this mountain, 'Be thou removed, and be thou cast into the sea;' and shall not doubt in his heart, but

4. shall believe that those things which he saith shall come to pass; he shall have whatsoever he saith.' Therefore I say unto you, what things soever ye desire, when ye pray, believe that ye receive them and shall have them." We must know that:

   a. Faith is the key that releases the resources of heaven into our situation.

   b. Faith must be put into action. You cannot say you believe in God and not put faith into action.

   c. Faith is not a trick performed with our lips, but a spoken expression that springs from the conviction of our hearts.

   d. Faith must be spoken. It is only when it is spoken that it begins to become active and effective toward specific results. (See James 2: 14 – 26).

We must believe God without doubting. We must believe that whatever the Lord says in His word is what He means.

5. Abide and pass the test. (Deuteronomy 8: 17 – 18.) Never say that it is by your own strength or power that you receive anything. Remember the wisdom, the anointing, everything that God gives you is for you to use to His honor and glory and for the building of His kingdom. It is for this reason we get wealth – for God's glory. Ensure that you guard

against Pride. Know that prosperity often brings arrogance. Know also that God is the source of all blessings.

6. Walk worthy. Colossians 1: 10

    a. Live a holy life. (Your lifestyle speaks volumes about you.)

    b. Do everything to please God, not man. For example, you must give performance at the highest level; be faithful in every task God gives you.

    c. Study the Word. Always seek to know more about God each day. Ask God to let you continue to be a student so that you can impart to others.

    d. Be committed to God's will.

    e. Know God for yourself.

7. Do not rob God! Not in any way at all! Pay your Tithes and Offerings and ensure that at all times, your time each day is not wasted but can be accounted for. Make good use of every moment of your day each day.

8. Proverbs 3: 9 – 10 says, "Honor the Lord with thy substance, and with the first fruits of all thine increase: So shall thy barns be filled with plenty,

and thy presses shall burst out with new wine." We must abide by this!

    a. Honor the Lord with everything.

    b. Once we get an increase, it belongs to God.

    c. You will not lack spiritually or financially.

9. Move fast with your assignment – the King's business requires haste. Jeremiah 1: 11 – 12 says, "Moreover the word of the Lord came unto me, saying, 'Jeremiah, what seest thou?' And I said, 'I see a rod of an almond tree.' Then said the Lord unto me, 'Thou hast well seen; for I will hasten my word to perform it.'" To "be ready" means "watching, walking, hastening, anticipating; being sleepless, alert, and vigilant – on the lookout." Jeremiah 31: 28 reminds us that God promises to watch over his people with an intent to build and plant the almond in heaven. It blossoms early, watching diligently for the opportunity to bloom.

10. The blessings of the Lord makes one rich and he adds no sorrow to it.

    a. God blesses us because he wants us to be rich.

    b. God don't bless us and add sorrow with it.

    c. The anointing is for the kingdom of God to be blessed.

    d. Our blessing is not for us alone but for others too, the poor, needy, those brothers and sisters in want.

11. Be obedient to God. This is true discipleship. Psalm 23: 6 says, "Surely goodness and mercy shall follow me all the days of my life; and I will dwell in the house of the Lord forever". These are the benefits of obedience and discipleship. You will be blessed so that you won't want to dwell anywhere else but in God's house.

12. Luke 6: 38 encourages us; don't be afraid to give plenty.

    a. Obey the voice of the Lord when He tells us to give – don't question the amount.
    b. Give abundant prayers and worship to God.
    c. Give love to others.
    d. Give God works because you will be judged by the same measure.

13. Always sow abundantly in every way. II Corinthians 9: 6 – 7 encourages you to sow seeds, love, and do good works, when you are blessed. We must be a blessing to others – we must therefore, give of our talents and our substance. Pray for your leaders; give time to soul winning and counselling. By doing these things, you will receive from God.

Chapter 17

SEASONS TO WIN

During the Christmas season, many say they don't celebrate it because that was not the date Christ was born. Whether or not that is so the date is irrelevant. The focus of Christmas Day is the fact that He came. He is the True Light that shines in this dark world.

Isaiah 9: 6 – 7 tells us, *"For unto us a Child is born, unto us a Son is given; and the government will be upon His shoulder. And His name will be called Wonderful, Counselor, Mighty God, Everlasting Father, Prince of Peace. Of the increase of His government and peace there will be no end, upon the throne of David and over His kingdom, to order it and establish it with judgement and justice from that time forward even forever. The zeal of the Lord of hosts will perform this."*

The four-fold name and attributes of the Child (Messiah), who was born to reign forever upon the throne of David, are given:

Wonderful, Counselor - (which express His ability as a Political Guide and a Leader; and that He is the Living Word, the infallible source of guidance, His in exhaustible Wisdom, the Truth and the Way.) On Him will rest the government, which is the entitlement of rule!

Mighty God - He is infinite and He is our Hero – because He as the Divine Warrior triumphs over sin and death for us!

Everlasting Father - He expresses Fatherly care toward us while being Omnipresent and Eternal.

Prince of Peace – the only One, Most High, Who can bring Peace!

Many are fighting globally, particularly the Secular 'religion', to put Him out of the season, while they condone Halloween and the celebrations of other gods.

Interestingly, at Christmas, many go through different moods – some are happy and some are sad because their loved ones are not around. Some are sick and unable to share in the happenings, others go through a myriad of emotions!

Growing up, Christmas was very exciting to me. I will never forget what was called Grand Market! Many gathered in the marketplace and sold all kinds of Christmas treats, toys and foods that were only prepared at that time of year – many recipes from generations prior. Also, those within the community many were given work – an opportunity to earn some money for Christmas. People would "white-wash" stones, tree trunks and the entire community had a sense of unity during the season. At that time, Jingle Bells and Mary's Boy Child by Boney M were in constant play! The Jamaica National Building Society would host *Greetings Across the World* on the television and the entire community would be at a standstill to see if any of their family members overseas would send Christmas greetings to them on television!

Everybody would be looking for Christmas Bonus. The farmers would be looking for bonus from the sales of their Chocolate and their Cocoa. Offices would give their faithful staff bonuses and staff awards! The managers would "let down their hair" for the staff to see the other side of them, and their children would come on site and mingle with the staff. It was a time of love – people showed love and it was more than just focusing on the market to make super-profits!

Show Some Love

God is Love, and we need to show some love each Christmas – one of the main seasons in which He is highlighted.

- ✓ *All businesses should give retired public servants – including teachers, police personnel, soldiers – major discounts during this season; at least 50%*

- ✓ *Workplaces should cut down on office parties and give Educational Vouchers to school-aged children of their staff.*

- ✓ *Supermarkets should issue groceries to the elderly within the communities they serve and pampers to the babies.*

- ✓ *Give the hardworking police personnel and soldiers grocery vouchers to pick up groceries.*

- ✓ *Distribution and Marketing Companies should give out gift baskets – especially to some of the university students – especially to those who are from overseas and find it difficult at this time of the year.*

✓ *Families who have a little more can share that extra with a family that does not! Go over and bring something to them for dinner!*

✓ *This is the time that the government should pardon some small crimes prisoners who are on good behavior. Show some love to them too.*

✓ *The media should lead a food drive this season – particularly in the rural areas that are generally forgotten!*

✓ *Don't forget to share with or give to your Pastors, during Christmas. They who labor with you and pray fervently for you and your family members!*

✓ *During Christmas, don't give up on the promises of God for which you are believing God! Hold on to your faith! Change is coming! Declare favor upon your life each day! God gives favor! Help someone, regardless of how small it is; it is a seed into your future!*

May you all experience the blessings of the Christmas season as you extend to others!

Consecration for Resurrection Blessing

The Resurrection season is the heart of our Christian faith, and it is critical for us all, not just Christians, to understand what it all means.

Because of the nature of this season, there are many blessings we can receive. First and foremost it is a time of hope -which is a powerful blessing. It means visions forgotten or lost can be restored. It means you can dream again and things that laid dormant can spring forth again, because of the sacrifice of Jesus Christ; that includes health, family and even your finance. Many have given up hope; but this Resurrection season is an opportunity for restoration and resurrection on all levels. Our hope is in Jesus Christ, and He is calling us to a place where the barriers and boundaries can be removed, that we can receive the benefits that are in store for us.

There are certain blessings that are impossible to receive without consecration. Consecration and Holiness is not being preached in many churches today, but it does not mean it is no longer required. There are 2 significant offerings which are mandatory for every Christian – Sin Offering and Trespass Offering. As is outlined in Exodus 19: 5 - 6 and in I Peter 2: 4 - 10, we as believers, are the only people on the face of the earth who God refers to as a treasure and as royalty to Him. In order to receive the coming wealth transfer that God wants to bestow upon His people, we must consecrate ourselves. There are many believers who will change churches every six months in pursuit of prosperity. It is not the church you are a part of -if you are not prospering then the time has come for you to examine yourself. Sin has placed a boundary before us as is stated in Exodus 19; and God wants to dwell with and fellowship with His people, but it takes a consecrated lifestyle. We must be set apart from the things of the world – the norms. We cannot be consecrated as a holy nation without the Blood of Jesus and only a consecrated life can be transformed. Sadly, many are comfortable conforming. It is even sadder that many Christian churches no longer preach/teach about the Blood of Jesus. Everything is in the Blood – life, healing, hope, deliverance and so much more! The shed Blood of Jesus makes it all possible.

Consecration Is Vital

The reason we are having so many problems – Crime, Violence, Poor Economy, Evil Cycles –is that despite the fact that God's people are praying for change, the people and the leaders are not consecrated. Isaiah 58 showed that the people were only fasting and praying to be heard while they turned a blind eye to the fatherless, the poor and the widow, and God said He could not answer their prayer. Isaiah 58 gives the dos and don'ts for God's people. Many Christians amass wealth and yet become so wicked and greedy; and they are quite vocal in the society – as if they really care.

Only a consecrated lifestyle can be sensitive to God's voice, will and purpose. There are too many people making poor decisions or are involved in sin, and are saying God has sanctioned it. He didn't.

The Benefits of Giving

Let us be reminded of the benefits of giving. When you give unto the Lord during the Resurrection Season:

- ✓ God will assign an angel to you. (Exodus 23: 20 & 23)

- ✓ God will be an enemy to your enemies. (Exodus 23: 22)

- ✓ God will give you prosperity. (Exodus 23: 25)

- ✓ God will take sickness away from you. (Exodus 23: 25)

- ✓ God will give you a long life. (Exodus 23: 26)

- ✓ God will bring increase and inheritance. (Exodus 23: 30)

- ✓ God will give a special year of blessing, and what the enemy stole will be returned to you and protected by God from being overtaken. (Exodus 23: 29)

If you are desperate for change, give during this season and experience the major, positive changes that will take place in your life.

2 Corinthians 6: 16 – 7: 1 reminds us: "… As God has said: "I will dwell in them and walk among them. I will be their

God, and they shall be My people." Therefore "Come out from among them and be separate, says the Lord. Do not touch what is unclean, and I will receive you." "I will be a Father to you, and you shall be My sons and daughters, says the Lord Almighty." Therefore, having these promises, beloved, let us cleanse ourselves from all filthiness of the flesh and spirit, perfecting holiness in the fear of God."

Chapter 18

BE HEALED

Some may wonder why adversity happens. Despite what you see, do not be discouraged. Adversity often makes us wiser and stronger than before.

Many of us have had painful experiences in our lives – the tragic loss of loved ones, broken relationships, betrayals, and even injustice meted out to us. However, despite all the hurt and pain we experience, one thing remains true; one of the greatest gifts we have is life. Once we have life, God gives each of us the capacity to bounce back and rise again. Regardless of how indebted, hurt, or grieved you are, He is able to give you double (blessing) for your trouble.

Only God can make the crooked places straight, the rough places plain, heal the hurting and weeping, and give joy and peace even in troubling times. He gives peace in the time of storm.

When the Wind Blows

Psalm 46: 1 – 3 tells us that there will always be natural disasters at different times, but God reminds us that even during the times of hardship He is present with us. He lets us know in Psalm 46: 3 *"Though* its waters roar *and* be troubled, *though* the mountains shake with its swelling"* He is present with us. This is not only so when the physical storms blow, but also when the spiritual, mental and the emotional storms stir.

We must understand that:

- ✓ When the wind blows, many things happen. There is uprooting, exposure, shifting and changing of courses. Thereafter, we have to clean up the debris, and sometimes in the midst of that you will find things you never saw before that can be a blessing to you. You may even see new springs.

- ✓ When the wind blows, the sea is purged and things that were hidden before are then brought into full view.

- ✓ When the wind blows the hearts of people change and they become more concerned about their neighbors and lend a helping hand.

- ✓ When the wind blows, there are new opportunities and new direction that await.

- ✓ When the trees are uprooted, they make room for new trees to be planted and to spring forth.

- ✓ When the wind blows, not only are hidden treasures revealed, but things that were planted that should not have been planted are removed so that you can prosper.

God Is Your Tomorrow

When we **worry** about tomorrow, we are trying to do God's job. He is in control of tomorrow and He knows what HE wants to do for us tomorrow. (Matthew 6) He is in control so we shouldn't worry or be anxious.

Faith in God changes the situation we are going through. God can turn difficult and impossible situations into some of our greatest moments of blessings. Tomorrow is God's today. Lack and adversity can change in 24 hours – in the same way that hopelessness within a nation can change in an instant.

God can change ordinary to extraordinary, lack to plenty, broke to wealthy and indebted to debt-free in an instant.

Nothing is ever as bad as it first appears. Worry only increases your medical bills. Your endurance is the key to your success. (Isaiah 40: 31) When you increase your faith in God, He will increase in your situation. Always remain positive. Speak *life* to your situation. Create your future with your word. You never know – oftentimes adversity will allow us to relocate which opens the door for new provision and ne possibilities.

During our struggles you can develop new relationships and new friends.

Farmers, Private and Public Sectors

This kind of adversity that has recently taken place is an opportunity for the farmers and members of the Private and Public sectors to get back to basics.

- ✓ Business owners can reduce the prices of their stock – particularly the old stock.

- ✓ Distribution companies and supermarkets can donate stock that is close to expiry

- ✓ All Inclusive can prepare meals with the leftover food to give to the poor within the guidelines that govern them.

- ✓ Furniture stores can donate bedding to those in dire need

- ✓ Linen stores and manufacturers can donate bed linen to those in dire need

- ✓ Media houses can create greater awareness of the needs of the poor by developing an initiative for people to give to the poor and to the places of shelter. They can offer scholarships to the children of farmers who have lost a lot in the recent disasters.

- ✓ Start Tithing and give to the poor.

All these things don't take endless meetings and planning. Once you obey, you are going to see increase in sales, profits. They may even discover oil, gold and natural cures for illnesses – lupus, diabetes, cancer or HIV. This would take us out of the paths of international lenders.

Comfort my people, the best is still ahead.

Healing Requires Faith Not Logic

Nobody likes or wants to be sick, but as life happens - as technology and global pollution increase, things get more difficult and stress intensifies, our health comes under great attacks from all angles.

The question is, are all parties in the health industry especially pharmacologists and research scientists more interested in treating rather than curing?

Health Services are among the most lucrative industries and the most political. In fact, this is an issue I have been speaking on for years. Even prophecies God has given to help individuals and nations, as well as recommendations given have been ignored.

At the rate we are going, only the rich will be able to be offered healthcare.

God wants us to be healed more than we desire to be healed; so much so that while Christ was on earth, it was his number one ministry.

"When the sun was setting, **all** those who had any that were sick with various **diseases** brought them to Him; and He laid His hands on every one of them and healed them." Luke 4: 40

He even commanded the church to ensure that healing be their number one priority. (Mark 16: 18; Luke 9: 1) God even gives the gift of healing to individuals for them to administer to those who are sick. He created plants, leaves and herbs for mankind's health. With the amount of money each person spends during his/her lifetime to deal with the common cold alone, they could make Forbes' list of billionaires. The greatest wealth transfer from the rich to the poor is in the area of wealth – and this is the area wherein God wants to do His greatest work. This is why the church should no longer be afraid of the media, theologians, the medical sector and heretics to carry out the healing ministry.

The very symbol used in the global medical field – the two serpents and the rod – is inspired by Numbers 21 and John 8: 36. Further to this, it was Jesus who died for us to receive healing! In Numbers 21, Moses was teaching the people that looking up at the bronze serpent on the stick which represents us lifting up our faith in Christ for the defeat of the enemy of sickness.

Healing is not for the logical. You can be given several instructions like Naaman received to dip seven times; or like the woman who was operating in a broken health system but was forced to change her mind set in order to receive her healing as she put her faith totally in God.

God Can Heal In Many Ways

There are many ways God can heal us – through surgery, advice of medical doctors, through the laying on of hands by praying elders and mothers in the church. (James 5: 13 – 18) God can allow medicine to be used, He can heal you supernaturally; He can use bushes and plants (II Kings 20) He can instruct us to Fast for healing – 3-day or 7-day Fasting. We can be healed by giving to the poor. Many doctors speak about the power and benefits of Fasting. However, consult your doctor before engaging in a Fast.

Additionally, you can anoint yourself with oil – as is found in Exodus 15: 26. God promises physical, emotional and spiritual healing. One of His names is Jehovah Rophe, which means 'God is our Healer'. You can also receive your healing as you forgive! Wherever the greatest problem lies is where the greatest solution will be found.

Revelation 22: 1 – 2 and Ezekiel 47: 12 lets us know that the fruits and leaves of the tree are for the healing of nations. The Caribbean, Africa and other poorer nations need to open their eyes and begin to put plans in place- building labs, engage in increased agriculture, acquire machines, remove taxes from all medical equipment which will create many jobs for the regions! There will be great regret if we don't put these in place.

The United Nations' Sustainable Development Goal regarding Good Health and Well-being is one which countries need to work on achieving which will ultimately make a positive contribution to Poverty Eradication.

By His Stripes You Are Healed

"But He was wounded for our transgressions, he was bruised for our iniquities: the chastisement of our peace was upon him; and with his stripes we are healed." (Isaiah 53:5)

No one wants to be sick and it is God's will for us to be in complete health (3 John 2). God wants us to prosper in body, soul and spirit. While God will use doctors to bring corrections to our bodies when we are sick we must realize that He is our healer, He is our chief physician. That is why he shed his blood on the cross, to bring healing. I believe Jesus' number one ministry was His healing Ministry.

Matthew 9: 35 tells us, "Then Jesus went about all the cities and villages, teaching in their synagogues, preaching the gospel of the kingdom, and healing every sickness and every disease among the people."

God wants to heal us emotionally, physically and spiritually. Even from broken relationships, and rejection. Romans 10 tells us that faith comes by hearing, and hearing the word of God, if you believe that God can heal you, confess it, this is a step in the right direction to receive your healing. Exodus 15: 26 shows that God wants no sickness in our bodies, he wants us to obey him and when we obey him no sickness from the Egyptians will come upon us. Psalm 147: 3 reminds 'He heals the brokenhearted and binds up their wounds.'

Here are 10 simple things each one of us can do to claim our healing.

1. 3 Day Fasting (Isaiah 58:8)

2. Give to the poor (Psalm 41)

3. Tithe (Malachi 3:8-12)

4. Confess Isaiah 53:5, Psalm 103 and Psalm 91 over your life daily.

5. Drink a lot of water and anoint your body with oil as a point of contact which is scriptural.

6. Confess any sin, get rid of any un-forgiveness

7. Use the blood of Jesus over your body by speaking it in prayer. The blood of Jesus never loses power!

8. Listen to the voice of God and obey his instructions (Deuteronomy 28: 1-14)

9. Ask your pastors to lay hands on you and pray for healing (James 5: 14-16)

10. Seek medical advice and follow your doctor's instructions.

I decree and declare Psalm 103: 1 – 4 and Psalm 107: 20 over your life.

I decree and declare creative miracles into your body.

I decree and declare complete restoration of health, body, soul and sprit.

I decree and declare that the manifestation of God's goodness will take place in your life and you will recover good health.

I decree and declare that there will be testimony of God's healing power for everyone who has read this.

I decree and declare not just your health but also there will be healing in your finance, your marriage, your children, your community and everything the enemy has robbed you of, and you shall recover all.

God bless you.

Chapter 19

WINNER KILLERS

Pride: The Pitfall

The word Pride may fall into two categories. First, it refers to **'a feeling of honor and dignity.'** For example, when Jamaica's sports personnel do well at the Olympics and our national anthem plays, we beam with pride. When

our soldiers march on parade in their colors, it's a beautiful scene and we are filled with pride!

Sadly, however, what has been hindering the nation overall is the second meaning of the word Pride and that is **'arrogance; conceit; having too high an opinion of oneself.'**

This kind of pride is number one of the seven deadly sins of which the Lord speaks. He hates Pride. (Proverbs 6: 16 – 19) Pride is what brings defeat to most individuals, businesses and administrations; and it runs across every sector. One of the main reasons the nation is in its current state is *pride*! Why do you believe that the churches in this nation (or anywhere) and the political parties and personnel cannot be united? Pride! One person, group or party sees itself as better than the other!

Pride causes one to take one's eyes away from God and begin to focus on or admire oneself and one's so-called accomplishments! Pride causes one to begin to focus on one's beauty, intelligence, level of education and academic accomplishments, and create a platform or pedestal for oneself from which to look down on others. It says everyone else around me is an idiot! 'I am better than my leaders!' 'I can do the job better than those who supervise me!'

Pride makes people unable to handle a certain level of power. It deceives and blinds persons from seeing to who they really are, and even more so, it leads to rebellion, conspiracy and undermining!

Have you ever seen an old friend, classmate or co-worker after years apart, one who has probably achieved a great deal academically, or who has amassed a certain level of wealth, fame or popularity? After having seen you, they behave as if they barely know you, or are better off than you; and as you attempt to speak to them they either pretend not to know who you are or address you condescendingly. That too, is PRIDE!

Pride Stops Victories

In II Kings 5, there was a great Syrian general, honorable, noble and powerful! A distinguished man! But he had a grave need, because he was a leper. It was recommended to him by a seemingly insignificant Israeli servant girl to seek help of a particular man from her country. Having sought the help, the instruction was given to him, by way of a messenger, to dip seven times in a muddy river. Pride in him said, **'A person in my capacity should be addressed directly by someone on my level, not by mere messenger!'** Pride in him said **'Aren't there bigger, better**

rivers where I am?' Pride also said **'This instruction is rubbish, why should I have to do that to get help?'**

There are many in society that have serious problems and are seeking for solutions. They spend millions without results – all because of PRIDE! What seems to be rubbish or to be foolish – the things, places and even persons on which we look down are oftentimes the vessels of our blessings! Further to that, the places on which we look down within the nation are the areas from which the source of our civic pride comes! From the inner city areas in our nation come some of the greatest world class athletes, musicians and more! Maybe if the general had met the man before he received the instruction, he would have disregarded or walked away from his blessing as a result of his perception of the man!

Pride is one of the main reasons that Jamaica has not yet changed! (Proverbs 8: 13 – 16)

When Pride (Arrogance) is dealt with and replaced with humility, then (Civic) Pride will be restored to the fullest extent.

While it is unfortunate that the symbol of Pride (Arrogance) according to Job 41 – the crocodile – is one of the main features of our currency, we as a nation can rise above that and embrace humility despite national and personal achievements, so that (Civic) Pride increases among us!

Selfish Ambitions

The greatest hindrance to mankind in building and advancing a nation or an organization is the focus on 'self'.

The success of great reformers and visionaries of the past, is that they put others and the progress of others above self. For change to take place locally and globally, we need first to look at the 'self' that stands in our way:

- ✓ Self-centered
- ✓ Self-control
- ✓ Self-esteem
- ✓ Self-interest
- ✓ Self-made
- ✓ 'Selfie'
- ✓ Self-confidence
- ✓ Self-taught
- ✓ Self-absorption
- ✓ Self-reliance
- ✓ Self-Conscious
- ✓ Self-Sufficient

When we begin to allow God to deal with *"self"* and we begin to look into ourselves and see the need for change, then we will experience change. Nothing is wrong with the country, the problem is with the nation – that is, the people. Many times, people talk about a country or an organization being wicked; but the country or organization is not wicked, it is the people. Because of selfish ambition, our politicians would not unite to address the issues and put the nation/people first.

We are now seeing Britain now putting their policies, economic and immigration reforms together for the benefit of the people of their nation; meanwhile, Jamaica and the Caribbean are lagging behind because of 'self'. Some (on either side) say: 'If my Party or my favorite people are not leading then I will not support it. Likewise, the sleeping giant called the church, will not unite to bring change unless it is their favorite leader or their own organization or congregation leading the charge. Our selfishness/self-centeredness is blocking growth, hindering true prosperity and an entire generation is now suffering as a result.

James 3: 16 says, "For where envy and self-seeking *exist,* confusion and every evil thing *are* there."
Selfish ambitions bring disorder within society; and regardless of what measures or systems are implemented – body cameras, lie detectors and so on – we are only shifting it from one category of people to another.

Philippians 2: 3 – 4 says, *"Let* nothing *be done* through selfish ambition or conceit, but in lowliness of mind let each esteem others better than himself. Let each of you look out not only for his own interests, but also for the interests of others."

Even in the marketplace, those who have been given the opportunity and favor to make it, in turn become selfish and hinder another from emerging. They would prefer to put legislation and monopolistic measures in place to stop some new people from benefitting and developing for the betterment of the nation. There are even leaders who would rather die in office at the expense of the nation, rather than elevating others to run with the baton. They prefer to talk about longevity of their tenure and what records they can break.

On a global level, when we look at what is taking place in Syria – the death of thousands take place daily because leaders what to dominate and determine how powerful they are globally. They would prefer to see people die that to bring a peaceful solution to the table. Pride, arrogance and selfish ambition is what caused Nebuchadnezzar to be turned into a beast at the hand of God.

It was selfish ambition that led to Genesis 11: 4 – everybody wanted to build, but only to make a name for themselves. They wanted to build a system without God. They wanted the benefits of God without submitting to the rule of God. They wanted to create a lifetime legacy that would keep them in power. We are now seeing many empires crashing down because of the selfish ambitions of others.

Selfish Ambitions cause poverty and crime to increase, as there is great imbalance in the distribution of resources, nationally and globally. It is the 'Me, Myself and I Syndrome' at work.

When we begin to put the interest of others, the vision of a nation or organization above our own, or even compliment and esteem others above self, then significantly more will be achieved at every level. So, we need to teach our children at home from an early age, how to share and care about others, how to show favor and mercy to others and that no man is an island. We need to teach our children and young people, and remember ourselves, that we must necessarily care about what happens to another and to those around us near or far, known or unknown to us and to use our resources wisely so that we all experience progress.

Chapter 20

WINNING COMMUNICATION

Does God Communicate With Mankind?

From time to time people will say, *'Did God say so?'* or *'Did God speak?'* Others will say, *'God never said that to anybody; you're telling me what you think?'* or *'That is gibberish, nothing goes like that!'* Even better, *'God does not work like that.'*

So the question is, does God communicate with man? Only someone that is dead is unable to speak. Is God dead?

Any teacher, professor or leader of an organization will tell you that Communication is a two-way process, and is not complete without a response of some kind.

Many times we hear persons say, 'Something tells me I shouldn't do this' or 'My mind is telling me not to take this bus' or 'Don't go on the corner today'; only to realize that when you obey, something terrible that happened there, and you were saved from it. So, who spoke?

How God Speaks

God speaks in dreams and visions, (Genesis 20: 6; Matthew 1: 19 – 21) through the written Word, directly in a still, small voice – face to face or in dark speeches, (Numbers 12: 6 – 8; I Kings 19: 12) or He uses His servants to speak to you (those who serve Him faithfully). God will even use a donkey to speak to you. (Numbers 22: 24 – 27). He will use the elements (atmospheric conditions); and He will speak to you through your circumstances.

Job 33: 14 - 16 says *"For God may speak in one way, or in another, yet man does not perceive it. In a dream, in a vision of the night, when deep sleep falls upon men, while slumbering on their beds, then He opens the ears of men, and seals their instruction."*

God shows leaders various symbols, even in their dreams, to allow them to lead effectively. For example, Many of those who dispute the fact that God still speaks, are among the first to run to the Horoscopes, Psychics, Tarot Readers, Tea Leaf Readers or listen to old wives' tales. The question is, with whom are they communicating when they go there?

The very rainbow we see from time to time is communication from God, reminding us of the Covenant He made with man on the earth. (Genesis 9: 13 – 16)

The very color of the grass is often a reflection of what is happening in a nation. An animal's response to its instinct warns man about what is happening in the atmosphere. When certain ants begin to dig up the dirt, we realize that rain is coming. When we see the ants in a long line storing up their food, you know that there are hard times ahead. Before the Tsunami in Thailand (2006) all the animals ran to the hills and many wondered why; it was the sign of an impending disaster.

God speaks also to the meteorologists. (Matthew 16: 1 – 4) When God does something atmospherically, they are being given the message for the people through the weather. They report the weather and give forecasts, but they cannot discern the meaning of what they are seeing so they cannot accurately inform the people.

When people say God spoke to them, the first thing they will hear is that they are fanatics or that they are paranoid or even schizophrenic. Some engage in phone bugging, secret tape recordings and computer hacking to get information. They trust the computer more than they are willing to spend time and listen to God.

Our inability to hear God's voice can be costly. It causes us to make wrong choices, poor decisions, deception, defeat, delay and death. A number of politicians, Administrations and organizations are no more, because of their inability or refusal to listen when God speaks.

Hearing God's voice daily will bring growth, increase, promotion and blessing. It will also save lives. It is critical for all individuals and national leaders, before making any major decisions, to seek to hear what God is communicating about it.

Whatever deals, agreements, activities, policies, reformations, laws, constitutional changes, or moves there are to be made, we must listen to the voice of God first and know what He is saying about them, so we can make the right decisions for the benefit of all.

The Effect of Ineffective Prayers

"So I sought for a man among them who would make a wall, and stand in the gap before Me on behalf of the land, that I should not destroy it; but I found no one." (Ezekiel 22: 30)

With the recent uprising and turmoil now happening worldwide – the wanton murders especially of women and children; and the attacks against churches, and the security threats throughout the globe – many questions must be asked. Such as, with a nation that has the most churches per square mile, why does it seem as if darkness is getting the upper hand?

Let us look at our options. Many of those criticizing the church are attempting to 'legislate' God out of the schools, businesses and the affairs of the nation, while they ask the question 'Where is God?'

One cannot pray effectively in order to bring quick results if there is unforgiveness or wrong motives. We can't be effective in prayer if one is politically-biased; praying blessings for their party while they declare curses on the opposing party. Are we praying the perfect will of God? One cannot pray the perfect will of God if one does not even believe in the Holy Spirit. (Romans 8: 26 – 28)

For example, if one is going to pray, then it is important for one to know what the will of God is in or for a particular situation. Often times we pray but it hinders God from truly moving, because they don't know His will.

Are we praying and calling on the names of God, because each name carries different results. God has a name for every situation and it is critical for us to use the name that applies to the situation at hand. If we want to be effective intercessors then we need to listen to what God is saying.

Are we praying the Word of God? Sadly, less than 20% of the Christians don't know the Word thus they don't know their rights. Most are just interested about getting a prophetic word about material items.

Let us recognize also that effective prayer does not mean hosting a Prayer Breakfast or a Prayer Conference and inviting the guest speaker to give a nice speech and talk about his books. If we don't help the poor and have mercy and compassion (Isaiah 58) our prayers will not be answered.

In order to achieve effective intercession there must be unity, regardless of one's class/status or denomination. Most want people to support them but when others who they deem unworthy of their presence, they will not support. If one wants results, one must be broken in humility before God!

To be effective in spiritual warfare prayer, one must be disciplined and willing to Fast. One cannot be walking in rebellion. A tree that is uprooted and replanted every month would die a slow death. Skipping from church to church will make one ineffective.

Intercession for Your Nation

Every person is required to pray if you want change. We must pray that God will reveal to us what we are really fighting against. Each of us is a watchman, and a watchman must stand in the gap. Standing in the gap means to bridge or repair what is broken. We must pray that God will deal with the epicenter of the problems and deal with the holes in the wall. We must be committed and disciplined! We must always remember that the word **'Intercession'** in Hebrew is **'Paga'** – which means to collide with, to encroach upon, to drive out, to strike up against, to be violent against' and so there is a measure of determination, effort and force in intercession.

As one who intercedes for his/her nation, one must:

- ✓ *Be confidential*

- ✓ *Live holy – keep your conversations circumspect; and maintain openness and brokenness before God.*

- ✓ *The Church was called to be a light for all and a pillar to the society.*

When we pray, there must be some ground shaking. Effective intercession is not about our status, it is about our lifestyle. Hence, it is our duty to unite and begin praying if we want to live in peace and to have our children experience the peace; so that the will of God aligns with the earth. So that leaders make the right choices and not be deceived by the love of money; and that they will work in the interest of the poor and the suffering and not for selfish gain. They must know that each one of them is accountable to God.

Chapter 21

IDENTIFYING THE VALUE IN OTHERS

Luke 23: 39 - 43 says: "Then one of the criminals who were hanged blasphemed Him, saying, "If You are the Christ, save Yourself and us." But the other, answering, rebuked him, saying, "Do you not even fear God, seeing you are under the same condemnation? And we indeed justly, for we receive the due reward of our deeds; but this Man has done nothing wrong." Then he said to Jesus, "Lord, remember me when You come into Your kingdom." And Jesus said to him, "Assuredly, I say to you, today you will be with Me in Paradise."

The choices we make on a daily basis are the keys to life, change and deliverance. There were two thieves on crosses beside Jesus - one made the right choice and one mad the wrong choice. An innocent man was ridiculed, rejected, mocked, whipped, flogged and nailed to the cross. We see this happen on a daily basis today. We see people doing the same thing today to Jesus! They ridicule His existence, death and resurrection. Even personally as Christians, many are murdered, ridiculed and mocked for their faith. Some even wonder if, when they are carrying their cross, if they are cursed. But there is good news for all who suffered - HE IS RISEN! He has paid it all for us! For the sinners you have a choice - to believe and to receive Him. Don't let family, pride, money, sex, material things, cause you to make the wrong choice! He is giving each person an opportunity right now. Don't be like the thief who rejected Him.

Romans 10: 9 - 13 shows us the way to Salvation. Just say this little Prayer:

Lord I am a sinner, I believe in you as Lord and Savior. I believe in your death and resurrection, Come into my heart. Wash me with your blood and save me. I confess all my sins. And I ask you to accept me as your son/daughter. Amen!

That's it you are saved! Welcome to the Family

Value Within What You Call Garbage

Many times when plans, ideas or suggestions are made by some within the society, many quickly label what they don't understand as garbage. The greatest value is often found in the garbage, the dump, the reject pile. In some countries, it is almost impossible to get a job on a garbage truck as a collector. The greatest problem we have in society is that it is so set up that we are quick to throw some valuable things into the dump heap! Society needs to have more recycling hubs than they do garbage heaps! What I am speaking of is two-fold. I am speaking of the literal garbage and the human beings that are pushed aside and ignored. It is said that "One man's trash is another man's treasure." If society is going to change then we are going to need to get our hands dirty by sorting through the "garbage".

There are some expensive and antique furniture, valuable equipment and useful scrap items that can be found in the garbage and scrap yards. There are even some machines that are in use today that companies have stopped manufacturing but are still useful; and the parts can often only be found in the scrap yards!

Jesus showed us the importance of what we consider as waste, fragments or crumbs in the parable of the five (5) loaves and two (2) fishes, that for proper management of your economy with the small resources, there is greater value within the crumbs even after distribution takes place. After distributing the loaves and fishes, the team collected twelve (12) baskets of crumbs. The number 12 signifies **government**.

A nation will never realize its full potential unless we start to pick up the crumbs instead of trampling on them! Focusing on the large investors to restore an economy will only bring the nation further into problems and greater debt. Focus on what we call 'crumbs' will bring greater benefit within a nation.

Very shortly, the greatest place for investment in the garbage dump; and the greatest revival in terms of bringing solutions and change to a nation will come out of people who are labeled as such by society. In many countries, the garbage dump provides employment for some. Surprisingly, in what is called the inner city or ghetto, even in the homeless bring the greatest glory or fame within a nation.

Pricelessness in the Trash

Every area of society is important. I have always said that many times governments fail because they try to associate themselves with like-minded people only or people they consider specialists in a particular area who are failing! Unless, as in the book of Nehemiah, we rebuild the Dung Gate – a place to where we carry our filth. Many investors even tend to look only within the upper echelon of the community. But those within the communities which are run down and are falling apart will bring greater return on investment. There are artefacts, ancient relics and discarded but valuable items within the dump.

When God is going to restore a society, he raises up/deals with the dump first. If the dump was not a place of value, why would scrap metal be so expensive? Scrap brings new business! Even solutions that people have received to bring change - that may not fit within society's textbook formats and diagrams - have been rejected and the problems continue. If leaders would revisit their dumps, archives and file thirteens13) they would be surprised at what they find.

Search the Dump

Every household, organization or nation must have a proper storage or 'dump' site to place what they consider to be junk or trash. Then take time out to carefully search that site from time to time, you would be surprised to see what you find. You might find gold, antiques, paintings, silver, letters, articles and other items of great value that you never realized you had. Maybe some of the things you will find will stop you from spending/wasting money trying to find something new or from re-inventing the wheel because what you needed was already there in the 'dump'!

Even visions and policies that have never been executed or implemented could be found and will result in less stress if implemented! You may also find other items that can be given to a Humanitarian efforts.

If each person starts from within their household, to see what items of value they possess, they would be surprised. Nations can only go forward if they begin to search the 'dump' and see what value they can find in the 'garbage' that can help to move the nation forward.

There is a famine coming and only those who are willing to search and embrace the 'garbage' and see the value within it will be able to bring change.

Encourage Someone Today With A Smile

Regardless of one's status, there are many going through great problems and the challenges of life. But regardless of what we are going through, and particularly those who interact with the public regularly (if not daily), we still need to encourage each other on a daily basis!

You may be going through financial, health or family problems, but if you encourage someone on a regular basis, we will all be able to get through each day more hopeful than we were the day before. In Jamaica, there is a saying, 'Encouragement sweetens labor.' We need to put this into action and reap the benefits.

Realize that regardless of how pleasant a person may seem, something troubling may be going on inside and you may just be the one who can change the course of that person's day for the better! A simple smile, or a kind word on the job may increase production tremendously. It can also reduce stress and the volume of medication intake. It can cause them to bounce back and if that is so, then both employers and employees benefit significantly! Kind words can bring peace, healing, hope and positive change!

You may think that your situation is bad until you come across someone in a worse position. Then you will realize that there is hope for you yet. Never complain about your environment or circumstances. Always pray and give thanks! You may be complaining about your salary/pay. What about those who don't have a job? If you don't have a job and you are complaining, what about those who have no job and no home? You may be complaining about your husband or wife. What about those who just lost a spouse or the single persons who are lonely and are praying to be married? Some of you may be complaining about your size, height or skin color. What about those who are terminally ill and just want to live?

Social and Political Problems

Many are complaining about social and political problems within the nation. Things may seem bad until you visit some other country and realize that you have a lot for which to give thanks.

In some countries, there are not even basic human rights. A simple thing such as drinkable water is unavailable! In some places, there is no freedom of speech – particularly for women – and there is no religious tolerance! In Jamaica, even the most wicked murderer will walk with a New Testament Bible in hand; while in other places, you can't even be seen with a page from the Bible. There are some places where gender issues cannot even be discussed or entertained in the least!

When we refuse to show gratitude to God for what we have, where we are and where He has taken us from or when we fail to encourage or motivate one on a regular basis we will lose those things!

For everything you have been through, use those experiences to help encourage someone else. Encourage someone today, although you may need encouragement yourself! When you feel discouraged, find someone in a worse situation than you are! Find the street boys and motivate them. Tell them what you have been through and the hope they have! It may sound far-fetched, but one kind word could start Crime Reduction!

There are two things about us as a people that we must seek to change; we criticize everything and we don't forgive! But when you turn the negative criticism into positive action, and begin implementing changes we would be better off! We are excellent at fault-finding, but terrible at implementing positive actions! How many positive plans have been developed? And how many of those plans have been implemented?

If we don't change, then one day, our beautiful nation will be taken over by expatriates, our people will become the minority and all the strategic areas in the nation will be held by foreigners. All the resources will be pulled from our country. Borrowing cannot take us out of debt we must unite to make that happen!

Any action taken to bring change to our nation must be a positive one and it can start with one smile.

Things to Know About People

When you are on a mission, not everyone will go all the way. Many will drop out. Not everyone wants to sweat or gain pain – some just want to partake in the blessing!

1. It is better to go through hardship with the right people than enjoy blessings with the wrong people.

2. Never look for man's approval, look for God's approval

3. Oftentimes persons that man looks up to and esteem highly, God does not esteem highly; and the people that man despises and rejects, God desires to bless and promote.

4. If everyone speaks well about you, then something is wrong with your life.

5. Never judge something by the outward, but discern the heart. Remember, man looks at the outward appearance, but God searches the heart.

6. Whatever or whomever you trust in before God will bring shame curse and defeat. Blessing and prosperity will come when you trust God FIRST. (Psalm 118: 8; Micah 7: 5; Jeremiah 17: 5 – 9)

7. Always keep away from people who carry an angry countenance, a backbiting tongue, and those who gossip and slander. Gossip and slander will defile you and stop your blessing. They will do the same to you. (Proverbs 25: 23)

8. Never have confidence in unfaithful people. (Proverbs 25: 19)

9. Always avoid people who tear down their leaders (Spiritual or Secular) with their tongue.

10. Be careful of people who say one thing before your face and another behind your back!

God is calling each and everyone in this season to pray as never before. Reach out to someone and give a positive word daily. We are seeing selfishness, greed and power destroy the very fabric of the earth; but you can make a difference and be the change. Be true to yourself. Remember, there is a Creator.

Born To Win

BIBLIOGRAPHY

Hayford, J. W. et. Al., (2002). The New Spirit-Filled Life Bible. Thomas Nelson Inc.

https://www.biography.com/people/george-washington-carver-9240299

https://www.goodreads.com/author/quotes/2834066.Winston_Churchill

www.ingramcontent.com/pod-product-compliance
Lightning Source LLC
Chambersburg PA
CBHW051820090426
42736CB00011B/1571

9 781732 076204